2/24

Prayer as a Political Problem

Prayer as a
Political Problem

by
JEAN DANIELOU

Edited and Translated by
J. R. KIRWAN

SHEED AND WARD : NEW YORK

This is a translation of L'Oraison Problème
Politique (*Arthème Fayard, 1965*)

Nihil obstat: M. W. ASHDOWNE, S.T.D., PH.L., Censor
Imprimatur: ✠ PATRICK CASEY, Vicar General
Westminster, 18 May, 1967.
The Nihil obstat *and* Imprimatur *are a declaration that
a book or pamphlet is considered to be free from
doctrinal or moral error. It is not implied that those
who have granted the* Nihil obstat *and* Imprimatur *agree
with the contents, opinions or statements expressed.*

Library of Congress Catalog Card Number 67-21913
Manufactured in the United States of America

Contents

Foreword

THE question which this book presents to the reader is this: What will make the existence of a Christian people possible in the civilization of tomorrow? The religious problem is a mass problem. It is not at all the problem of an élite. At the mass level religion and civilization depend very much on one another. There is no true civilization which is not religious; nor, on the other hand, can there be a religion of the masses which is not supported by civilization. It would appear that today there are too many Christians who see no incongruity in the juxtaposition of a private religion and an irreligious society, not perceiving how ruinous this is for both society and religion. But how are society and religion to be joined without either making religion a tool of the secular power or the secular power a tool of religion? This book invites the reader to join in the search for an answer to this problem which is vital for tomorrow.

JEAN DANIELOU

I

The Church of the Poor

NOT all who today speak of the Church of the poor put the same meaning on the term. Indeed, one can see in the term two opposing conceptions of the Church. On one view, the Church stands before the world as a sign, giving witness in the world to that which surpasses the world. On this view, the essential thing is that the Church should bear witness and make sure of satisfying the first requirement for this, which is purity. Attempts are made to keep it clear of civilization lest its purity be compromised. There is a nostalgia for the times of the martyrs and talk of the end of the Constantinian era. To protect the Church's purity, those who hold this view would go so far as to risk the abandonment of the crowd of baptized Christians for whom Christianity is hardly anything more than an external routine.

In opposition to this view there is another which is beginning to make headway. This does not look back to and defend a Christianity embedded in history, but rather forward to what the Gospel itself calls for on a realistic view of the future. For those who take this view of the matter, the essential character of the Gospel is to be the religion of the poor—using that term not to indicate those who are detached from earthly things, but those who form the great mass of mankind. This view shares St Augustine's picture of the Church as a net in which all sorts of fish are caught, where the task of separating the good from the bad is for the angels, not for men. On this view of the matter, the Church was most truly itself in the days of Christendom when everybody was baptized and it is this state of affairs which is much to be desired. But this situation supposes a Church which is involved with civilization, for if civilization runs counter to it a Christian people cannot exist. This Church, a great crowd of saints and sinners intermingled, is found preferable as a Church to one which might be purer but would strongly resemble a sect.

What does seem to be clear is that the Gospel message is addressed to all men, and especially to the poor, and that the Church, the community of those who have received this message, is therefore open to everybody. This is stated clearly in the Gospel, where Christ applies to himself the words of Isaiah: "I am come to preach the Gospel to the poor." The word "poor" can have several meanings. It can mean those who are in poverty; and Christ then will comfort their misery. It can mean the poor in spirit, those who seek first of all

the kingdom and its righteousness, and will risk everything else to gain that. But it means also the undistinguished and unprivileged, those who lack money,
education, and rank. This is the sense in which we use
it here.

Christ's own actions support this meaning. We see
him in the New Testament followed by men of all
types. There were notabilities, such as Nicodemus and
Joseph of Arimathea, but there were also extortioners
and harlots. One notes in particular how Jesus scandalized the Pharisees when he refused to set any value
on the purifications prescribed by the law and sat
down to eat with whoever happened to be around. He
made it clear that faith alone gives entry to the kingdom. Further, although Jesus selected and trained a
small band of disciples in the first part of his ministry,
he also spoke to the multitude. And the Gospel says
they followed him. Then there is the way in which
Jesus welcomed children—which, as Cullmann has
shown, expresses the simple sense of community.

That this universalism is one of the marks which
distinguishes the Church is shown again by a study of
the early Christian centuries. Most remarkable evidence of this is given by the pagan Celsus condemning
the Christian communities as packs of vagabonds and
pointing by contrast to the Pythagorean brotherhoods
recruited from the intellectual and moral élite. Nor can
we oppose the pre-Constantinian era to the Constanti-

nian in this particular. By the third century, in Africa and in Alexandria, we have Cyprian and Origen complaining that an increase in numbers brings with it a loss of fervour. Moreover, we know that the persecutions were sporadic and of limited duration.

This much only is true—the extension of Christianity to an immense multitude, which is of its very essence, was held back during the first centuries by the fact that the social cadres and cultural forms of the society in which it operated were hostile to it. To cleave to Christianity called then for a strength of character of which the majority of men are not capable. When the conversion of Constantine removed these obstacles the Gospel was made accessible to the poor, that is to say, to those very people who are not numbered among the élite. The man in the street could now be a Christian. Far from distorting Christianity, this change allowed it to become more truly itself, a people.

It is this Christian people which exists today in Brittany and Alsace, Italy and Spain, Ireland and Portugal, Brazil and Colombia. It is this people which feels itself betrayed by those groups of Catholics, clerical and lay, whom it sees as more concerned with dialogue with Marxists than with work for its defence and growth. Of course missionary work is essential, but St Paul asks us to think also of those who are our brothers in the faith. It would be criminal if the crowd of poor confided to its care were abandoned on the pretext that the Church could do more effective missionary work without them. It is this Christian people which has stood firm in Russia against the Marxist ideology. It is this people that the persecution now going on seeks to destroy. And that is why this persecution is particularly hateful, for it seeks to destroy that most sacred thing, the faith of the poor.

The modern drama of Western Christianity, of that part of the world, that is to say, where a Christian people has existed, lies precisely in this, that the masses are being dechristianized. Of course there are crises among the intellectuals, but that is nothing new. It is no more dangerous for a Christian country to have in its midst a few atheistic intellectuals than it is for an atheistic country to have in it a few Christian intellectuals. It is much more serious when a Christian people is destroyed, for it can be built up again only after a long and patient effort.

Our task, therefore, is to discover what those conditions are which make a Christian people possible. To do that we have to ask what conditions have in fact made a Christian people possible. And what we may find, strangely, is that those who speak most of the evangelization of the poor are often those who fight hardest against the conditions which make the Gospel accessible to the poor.

We can begin with one of the best established findings of contemporary missionary theology. Christianity is on the retreat in the old colonial countries and particularly in the Far East. A major cause of this is that Christianity had become tied to its Western forms and was not incorporated into the systems of thought and art and manners of those countries. Christianity came to seem alien to national traditions. Its future becomes precarious because conversion acquires the smack of treason and becomes a difficult thing, at best forcing a man on to the fringe of the life of his country. We see now that before the faith can be truly rooted in a country it must penetrate its civilization and bring into existence a Christendom. Christianity is accessible to a people as revelation only when it is rooted in that people as religion.

Thus contemporary pastoral theology confirms the legitimacy of the Constantinian process. It was because from the fourth century Christianity had penetrated Western civilization and formed a Christendom that the immense Christian people of the medieval West became possible. Of course, this people had the defects common to all people. For many, Christianity was less a personal engagement than a social tradition, less a supernatural faith than a religious need. But is it not desirable, we should ask, that the Gospel should be taken even to such poor as these, who do after all receive something of its saving power?

14

Such is indeed the problem which the pastoral care of the masses poses. Experience shows that it is practically impossible for any but the militant Christian to persevere in a milieu which offers him no support. Think of the many who attend service in their villages but cease to go once they live in a town. Are we then to speak of sociological Christianity and conclude that it is better to be rid of Christians such as these? It would be entirely wrong of us to do so. The Christianity of these Christians can be real, while yet not personal enough to prevail against the current. Such Christians have need of an environment that will help them. There can be no mass Christianity outside Christendom.

There lies the choice. Among those who will say that Christianity does not need a great following, that it is better to have only a few Christians who are fervent than many who are not, there are some who will add that the Gospel demands are clearly beyond the capability of more than a small number of people. Christianity, they will say, should be content to be the leaven and the salt and for that reason take care to avoid being mixed in with the dough. The one thing essential for it is to keep its savour. The Church is a sign set up in the midst of the peoples. Her solicitude should be rather to remain intact than to recruit large numbers of members. Besides, only God knows who is to be saved. There are different ways in which people can belong to the Church. What the Church should do is to remain faithful to herself.

That there is much that is true in this argument cannot be denied. Nevertheless, it is unacceptable. Certainly, it is true that only a chosen few will ever fully satisfy the requirements of the Gospel; but does it follow that the Church should number no more than this élite? Is it not essential that all men who put their faith in Christ should belong to the Church? Is it not a matter of some importance that a man should express his fundamental religious need in the Christian way? Is it not essential that the Church be everywhere present as an institution in her teaching and her sacraments so that all may come to her and take from her what they can? Otherwise, is there not a danger of turning Christianity into a sect and a religion for intellectuals?

The Church has an absolute duty to open herself to the poor. This can be done only by creating conditions which make Christianity possible for the poor. Therefore there is laid upon the Church a duty to work at the task of making civilization such that the Christian way of life shall be open to the poor. Today there are many obstacles standing in their way. In a technological civilization men tend to be absorbed in care for material things. Socialization and rationalization leave little room for a personal life. Society is so disordered that large numbers have to live in a poverty which makes a personal life impossible. The result of the secularization of society is that God is no longer present in family, professional, or civic life. A world has come into being in which everything serves to turn men away from their spiritual calling.

It is sufficiently clear that Christians ought to be trying to change the shape and pattern of society so as to make possible a Christian life for the whole of mankind. It is also obvious that such a transformation must in any case be slow and may sometimes be ruled out by circumstances. However that may be, somehow a start has to be made, and this can be done by creating oases in the prevailing secularism where the Christian vocation can develop. This thought inevitably raises the question of those Christian institutions which provide services not of themselves within the Church's competence, but which the Church might be brought to provide: schools, unions of employers and of workers, etc., which bring Christianity into social life not merely at the level of individual witness but at that of a community.

In doing this sort of thing the Church lays claim to nothing that any religious body could not lay claim to. Religious freedom must be thought of as a right that belongs to communities as well as to individuals. It implies not only that people should be able to practise a religion publicly, but also that they should have the scope and mutual support necessary to order their lives in accordance with the demands of that religion. In no other way can a tradition be kept alive among a people. Hence, a religion has the right to set up at the family, educational, cultural, and social levels those institutions of which it has need to ensure its continuance and development.

It is in this perspective that the need for relations between Church and public authority becomes evident. This question is often put on a false basis because it is looked at in a mistaken way. It is seen in the light of conditions which obtained in the past, when because the Church enjoyed privileges in certain States she found herself entangled in their political and social structures. The overthrowing of these temporal structures leaves behind sociological factors which are so many obstacles preventing the Church from carrying out her mission. This explains why some Christians, rejecting as "sacral" societies those which have an association between the two, call for a radical separation of ecclesiastical from civil institutions.

This position is explicable, but none the less false and dangerous. It fails to recognize the fundamental fact that religion of itself forms part of the temporal common good. Religion is not concerned solely with the future life; it is a constituent element of this life. Because the religious dimension is an essential part of human nature, civil society should recognize in it a constituent element of the common good for which it is itself responsible. Therefore, the State ought to give positive recognition to full religious freedom. This is a matter of Natural Law. State atheism, which stifles religious life, and laicism, which ignores it, are both contrary to Natural Law.

Furthermore, in a socialized society, as ours is becoming more and more, it is certain that recognition by the State of religious communities as real aspects of public life is a necessary condition of their existence both as communities of the poor and as religious groups. In a capitalist society religious communities were able to find private sources of provision for their material needs. This had two defects. In the first place, it tied them to the power of money; and secondly, it led them to seek their recruits for the most part from the leading social groups and to keep themselves apart from the poor. In a socialist society the position is different. Recourse can be had less and less to private funds, and institutions will be able to survive only to the extent they are recognized and supported by the State. It is strange that it should be often the same Christians who advocate both socialism and laicism, for the two sets of ideas are contradictory.

In arguing in this manner we stand firmly on the Natural Law. The argument is not that the civil authority should recognize Christianity as such, but that it should recognize religious institutions in general because religion is a social fact. It is not to be supposed that the civil authority has competence of itself to decide upon the truth or otherwise of a religion. That to which it is bound by Natural Law is to recognize the reality of religion under whatever form that reality shows itself at any given time and place.

It is evident that the problem of the relationship between Church and State shows itself in different ways at different times. The problem today is not the same as it was in medieval civilization. That civilization was characterized by the recognition by the State of the Catholic religion in preference to all other religions, whether pagan or Jew. The State was denominational rather than sacral. The Church enjoyed privileges from which other religions were debarred. It has to be recognized, of course, that this was the usual state of affairs at the time. It was not possible then to dissociate the State from a particular religion.

The question of religious liberty is completely different. Of course, the Church does not surrender any of the sovereign rights of the truth which is in its charge. That is not at issue. The principle on which religious liberty rests is that not only are individuals not to be prevented from following their consciences in religious matters, even if they are in error, but also they are to have the right to group themselves into communities and ask for whatever is necessary for their continuance and development. Religious liberty, in other words, has no meaning unless it is concrete, unless, that is, the material conditions for its existence are assured. In a socialist world such assurance can be given only by the State.

Those who look at the matter in terms of historical situations are usually unable to see clearly into the question of the relations between Christianity and civilization. For them, insistence upon these relations appears to spring from a wish to keep Christianity involved in the structures of an outworn world. Therefore, they see a demand for separation as an expression of a wish to face up to new circumstances. In terms of history they have reason on their side. The relation of Christianity to civilization is made up perpetually of breakings apart and joinings together again. When they speak in this sense of freeing Christianity from a certain sociological burden they are saying something meaningful.

However, it is quite another thing to transpose these historical perspectives to the theoretical level. It is unreal and dangerous to accept separation as a concept of any value, to oppose a secular to a Christian civilization, to consider that the Church and the civil society ought to move in two separate worlds. It is dangerous for the Faith, for it can be the faith of the poor only if civilization makes it easily accessible to them and does not make it a privilege for a chosen group of spiritually-minded people. It is dangerous for the civil society, for it leaves that society to shape itself in an incomplete and inhuman manner. That is the problem with which we are faced.

II

Prayer as a Political Problem

THE reader might well be surprised by the title given to this chapter and this book. Public policy and prayer are two realities not usually brought together in this way. I have chosen the heading deliberately, because it seems to me essential to make it clear—perhaps somewhat provocatively—that there can be no radical division between civilization and what belongs to the interior being of man; that there must be a dialogue between prayer and the pursuit and realization of public policy; that both the one and the other are necessary and in a sense complementary. In other words, there cannot be a civilization within which prayer is not represented; besides, prayer depends on civilization.

There is another reason for this title. For me it points also to the fact that we live at a time when many barriers that we are accustomed to see erected between different spheres of human existence are being swept away. It is being borne in upon us that we have to start again and reconsider the whole problem of man at grips with the world. Today, we only have use for thinking that is bold enough to free itself from the detritus of history and face up to the real problems of the future. In one sense, we have need of prophecy. Hence the importance of the witness of such men as Teilhard de Chardin and La Pira, men who break out of the narrow compartments into which we seek to segregate human problems and try to deal with them in their full extent.

The way in which the problems of religion and civilization depend upon each other is shown most clearly in the difficulties experienced in the spiritual life of contemporary man. We all feel that spiritual experience, prayer, is in danger today. For us, who consider that man's relationship to God is an essential part of human nature, and for whom there can be no civilization unless adoration finds a place in it, this problem is a vital one.

By prayer in this connection I mean spiritual experience orientated towards God. There are two aspects of the question I shall ignore. First, I say nothing of any spiritual experience which could be simply a man's awakening to consciousness of himself; for in this sense, spiritual experience could have an a-religious significance, being simply a beginning of self-consciousness. Second, I do not consider prayer in its specifically Christian sense; for I treat of it firstly as a constitutive part of all religions, being their interior aspect, and secondly as in itself a fundamental part of all humanism.

Prayer cannot exist in the abstract. It can exist only as the act of a particular man at grips with life. So it requires those conditions which alone will render it possible for the majority of men. These conditions can be seen as a function of man's balance in soul and body, and spiritual experience can be assigned its place in the complete life that such balance gives. Civilization is a conditioning factor. The prayer of modern man is that of one caught up in the world of technical civilization, with all the profound change which that brings to the rhythm of human existence. The problem which faces us, therefore, is that of the future of prayer in technical civilization.

So much for what I mean by prayer. Now as to what I mean by politics. In this context I mean by politics the sphere of the temporal common good. This covers three things.

In the first place, we are dealing with man collectively and not with the individual. We shall be speaking, therefore, of the prayer of man involved in social life. It is in this sense that prayer belongs not to the strictly interior life of man—with which politics has nothing to do—but to the political sphere.

Secondly, politics ought to have the care of the common good, that is to say, the duty of creating an order in which personal fulfilment is possible, where man

25

might be able completely to fulfil his destiny. Jeanne Hirsch says: "Politics is not in itself creative, but it does provide the conditions in which something can be done." This is one of the best possible definitions. If politics does not create the conditions in which man can completely fulfil himself, it becomes an impediment to that fulfilment.

Finally, we are dealing with the temporal and not the eternal good. I shall be speaking of prayer, therefore, not in so far as it is an anticipation of eternal life in us, but in so far as it forms a constitutive part of the whole temporal order, of earthly civilization in the full sense of the word. Now the temporal order, it will be admitted, includes within it the realm of material goods—and it is the very first task of politics to assure to all men the material conditions necessary to their existence. Politics has also another purpose—to make a world in which human relations can flourish in freedom, that is to say, a society in which man does not exploit man, from which racism of every sort is banished, where understanding is open, and peace between nations becomes possible.

But politics limited to these objectives would still not assure a complete temporal common good. I agree with La Pira in his statement—and I have often quoted this—that the true city is that "in which men have their homes and God also has his. . . ." A city which does not possess churches as well as factories is not fit for men. It is inhuman. The task of politics is to assure to men a city in which it will be possible for them to fulfil themselves completely, to have a full material, fraternal, and spiritual life. It is for this reason that we consider that, in so far as it expresses this personal fulfilment of man in a particular dimension, prayer is a political problem; for a city which would make prayer impossible would fail to fulfil its role as a city.

So I shall speak of prayer as a social problem. Here again there are some points on which we must be clear. To say that prayer is a social problem might seem in itself to be paradoxical. Prayer is a personal relationship with God. Does it not, therefore, belong strictly to personal life? It is true that it does, but it is true also that the full development of this personal life is impossible unless certain conditions obtain. To deny this would be to fall victim to that most detestable form of idealism which separates spiritual existence from its material and sociological substratum. It is our profound belief that man is a unity; that is to say, that there is a fundamental connection between the problems of the body and those of the soul. (It may be that we are still even today victims of a twisted system of morals that refuses to take the findings of biology into account.)

Just as man is a creature of flesh, and the work of prayer cannot be considered in him independently of the fact of his body; so he is also a social being, and cannot fulfil himself in prayer divorced from his social nature. At this point there are two things to be said. In the first place, for some individuals a life of prayer is always possible, whatever the circumstances. No matter where they are, or under what conditions, their personalities are strong enough to develop their powers without help from their environment, or even in spite of it. In the second place, there is the special case of those who withdraw from society in order to lead a spiritual life. I shall not be speaking of them; although I might mention that monks, in fact, create for themselves the environment in which they can pray effectively.

It is this last consideration that brings us to the heart of our problem. If monks feel the need to create an environment in which they will find prayer possible, if they think that prayer is not possible without certain conditions of silence, solitude, and rule, what are we to say of the mass of mankind? Should prayer be the privilege of a small spiritual aristocracy, and should the bulk of the Christian people be excluded from it? The problem with which we are faced is the problem of prayer for everybody, of the possibility of prayer for men at grips with the realities of the temporal life as it is lived today, whether in the family, at work, or in the city. This is what we are up against and in the end it is the only problem that really matters.

We must react against any view that makes spiritual

life the privilege of a small number of individuals; for such a view betrays the essential point of a message which is not only Christian but religious, that a life of prayer is an absolutely universal human vocation. Quite apart from the teaching and demands of Christianity, there is the simple fact that prayer is a constitutive element of human life. All religions attest this. This was taken for granted by Christ when he addressed his message to the poor—giving to that word the meaning we have already attached to it: all and sundry, the undistinguished and unqualified, the men in the street.

We ought never to forget that the Church is the Church of Everyman. The salvation which Jesus Christ comes to offer, the life which he comes to give, are salvation and life offered to the poor—to all—and what is offered to all must be within the reach of all. Yet today, for most men, given the circumstances in which they find themselves, the realization of a life of prayer is practically impossible. It is evident that society is deformed. It is deformed not only because there are some men who lack bread, nor only because there are human relationships that lack honesty, but also because this world of prayer which is an essential element in man himself cannot expand and grow.

There is one further point to clarify. I am speaking of prayer in so far as it is bound up with particular social conditions. What I want to say by this is that religion ought in fact to have a social character. Religion as a fact supposes an environment in which it can develop. There are two dimensions in religion which ought always to be considered as complementary. When religion becomes a purely social fact we fall victims to a sociological Christianity which consists of certain gestures, practices, and traditions; and this is totally insufficient. Sociological Christianity ought always to be tending to transform itself into personal Christianity; religious practices ought always to be tending towards prayer, the interior attitude tending always to correspond to the external gesture. But the opposite is equally true. There cannot be a personal Christianity unless there is also a social Christianity. If personal religious life is to be able to flourish, it must have a certain minimum of help from outside, for without this it is normally impossible for the majority of men.

This point must be stressed, because some people today tend to dismiss the idea of sociological Christianity. They usually do so under the illusion that this is a matter of keeping to particular sociological forms of Christianity which are tied to outmoded forms of civilization. (This could in fact be happening in some traditionalist countries, where a sociological context helps to maintain religious life, but at the same time acts as a brake on the development of humanity.) No, what is important is that, with an eye to the future, we take account of the fact that certain sociological conditions have to be realized if the life of prayer is to be accessible to all and sundry. If we fail to do this and detach spirituality from its collective context, we shall be neglecting reality. It is against such a dissociation as this that we ought to react.

The civilization in which we find ourselves makes prayer difficult. The first thing that strikes one is that our technological civilization brings about a change in the rhythm of human existence. There is a speeding up of tempo which makes it more difficult to find the minimum of freedom on which a minimum life of prayer depends. These are elementary problems, but none the less basic. Prayer is thus rendered almost impossible for most men, unless they display a heroism and a strength of character of which—we must face it—the majority of men are not capable. If it is only the shelter of a rule which makes possible the flowering of a life of prayer for professed religious, then the laity, without this shelter and with added obstacles, must indeed be in difficulties. Shall we say that the life of prayer can be possible only for those who are able to take advantage of such shelter and thus restrict it to only a small part of humanity?

To be a man of prayer, some might say, it is not necessary to consecrate certain times to prayer; men can find God in everything. This is perfectly true.

Prayer as a Political Problem

Nevertheless, we begin to be able to find God in everything when we have begun by finding him above and beyond everything. It is practically impossible to lead a life of union with God so long as there has not been that minimum of formal prayer which allows us to acquire spiritual liberty by accustoming us to disengagement from the chains of our environment. I could cite numberless witnesses in support of this thesis. Let me repeat, these matters cannot be discussed in the abstract: the problem must not be put theoretically, but concretely, taking the facts of our lives into account.

Thus we have a problem of rhythm, of the pace of time. We also have the problem of the socialization of our lives. Even as prayer has need of a certain minimum of time, so also it has need of a certain minimum of solitude, a minimum of personal life. In the actual conditions in which men have to live today, this is practically impossible. Urban life sucks people up into a relentlessly collective existence. Père Depierre once said that one of the reasons why working men went to the cinema was to seek silence and solitude. It was only there that they could be free of the necessity of replying to all the demands that were forced upon them, from the moment they began work in the morning to the time when they went home in the evening to their families. The man of today is an alienated creature, one who has lost the possibility of finding himself, who no longer knows who he is, who has had to meet this never-ending barrage of demands from outside himself and who has ended by becoming depersonalized.

The problem with which we have to deal here is not simply that of prayer. In a more general manner, we are concerned with the possibility of personal existence. This is not a problem for only the religious man alone. It is of interest to all men, for all are threatened with becoming mere units in a collective existence. It is obvious that some measure of solitude is essential for prayer to the extent that prayer is the meeting of faith and spiritual experience, the possibility, that is, for faith to become really part of a man. To the extent that faith fails to become an inner part of man, it tends to be nothing more than an external practice; and this is the danger that now threatens.

Another kind of question arises out of this process of "desacralization" which is now going on in our technological civilization, at least in its present stage. Here we touch on very important and very delicate problems, matters on which Christians themselves are divided, but with which it is absolutely essential to deal. The civilizations of the ancient world were sacral; that is to say, they were civilizations in which the framework of human existence had an ultimate religious foundation. That was true of all of them, of the Greek and Roman as also of the Jewish world. It was

33

true also of all the animist societies of Africa and Oceania. It is still true today of the Moslem world. It is evident, however, that technological civilization and the phenomena it brings in its train (urbanization, for instance) break into and overthrow the old social cultures, separate profane culture from religious life, and destroy a certain balance between the social and the religious dimensions of man.

The gravity of this crisis for religion and the State must not be minimized. When collective existence was impregnated with religious values there was formed a world in which the very framework of living provided a constantly renewed contact with sacred things. In its traditional form that state of affairs could not survive the irruption of technological civilization. The West suffered the shock first and has still not recovered from it. Until only a short time ago the study of the Koran was the foundation of the culture taught at the University of Fez. Today, the culture which the young Moroccan students want is the technological culture of the West. Moslem youth, who must pass from a stage of civilization which is still sacral to the condition of contemporary civilization, is therefore facing a deep crisis.

One particularly grave aspect of this problem, and one in which our responsibilities are immense, is the irruption of technological civilization into emergent countries such as Madagascar or the countries of

Africa. I have discussed these matters recently with a technician from those parts and I am myself terrified by our failure to grasp what is involved. We are aware that technical knowledge is in the process of destroying a whole civilization and we give no thought whatsoever to what is to be put in its place. Of course, it is no more possible to preserve the sacral African forms as they are now than it was to preserve the traditional forms of the Christian civilization. But this in no way detracts from our special responsibility today of finding how to make the religious dimension really present in technological civilization, working through the framework of society itself.

We come back always to the same thought. If that dimension remains completely absent from that society, if we accept a complete dissociation of the sacred and the profane worlds, we shall make access to prayer absolutely impossible to the mass of mankind. Only a few would be able to find God in a world organized without reference to him. Men move not only in their social environment, but in their cultural environment as well. It is through this cultural environment that they can have access to the realities of religion. A world which had built up its culture without reference to God, a humanism from which adoration was completely absent, would make the maintenance of a positive religious point of view impossible for the great majority of men.

Prayer as a Political Problem

There can be no questioning the value of the scientific approach, so long as it does not try to dabble in matters outside its competence. Our task is to find new ways by which the world of contemporary thought, and in particular the world of science, can become a pathway to God. In this connection I would like to recall something that was said by Teilhard de Chardin, in which he showed that for him—and this is one of the aspects of his work that I most admire—it was perfectly possible to take an optimistic view of the question. Teilhard wrote in *Sauvons l'humanité* : "As it arrives at a higher degree of mastery over self, the spirit of the world finds within itself a more and more pressing need for adoration. The fact of universal evolution makes God appear greater and more necessary than ever. Nothing could be more mistaken than to regard religion as a primitive and passing phase of mankind's infancy. The more man-like man becomes, the more necessary it is for him to know how to adore and to be able to do it. The fact of religion is an irreversible cosmic fact of the first magnitude."

This scholar's declaration of faith that the very progress of scientific evolution ought to bring a greater desire for adoration is one of the most magnificent professions of optimism I have come across. Continuing to use Père Teilhard's illustration, I would go on to say that while humanity's infancy is bound up with a particular type of sacral civilization, atheism does not represent the stage of humanity's adulthood. On the contrary, it represents its adolescence. It comes at that moment exactly when infant humanity revolts against the universe within which it is formed. We know that revolt is essentially an adolescent attitude. With adulthood, on the other hand, comes a higher equilibrium which permits recovery of the fundamental religious values in a new balance of forces.

Why is it that prayer is fundamental to politics? As I have already said, politics exists to secure the common good. An essential element of the common good is that man should be able to fulfil himself at all levels. The religious level cannot be excluded. Indeed, the possibility of self-realization at that level is a fundamental element in the common good. The State must make provision for it, for we cannot suppose that a true polity can exist where there is no room for the religious dimension. In the State there must be a place for both service and adoration. Simone Weil was right to protest against today's total secularization of society and the universe, and to insist that a constitutive element which keeps a civilization in balance is the fundamental relationship of society and the universe to all that is sacred.

We are aware today of the problem created by the absence of the religious element from the fabric of civilization. There is evidence in several directions that

science doesn't provide ends

equilibrium is endangered. Science, in particular, is totally unable to guide a movement which it has itself set in train. Men feel that science has sent them on a journey without benefit of steering wheel or brakes. So the question arises, for all men, religious or not, whether the development of technological civilization as such seems a sufficient response to the problem of a humanity in course of development; that is to say, whether this civilization either proposes ends which have any meaning, or provides standards by which progress can be measured.

This raises the question of the function of the spiritual domain within the world of technology. Attempts have been made to find an answer in some philosophy of man, a type of humanism, at the level of which some sort of human order could be established. It must be said that what has been done in this direction so far has not succeeded in finding a solution. A common humanism which could embrace men of all varieties of spiritual allegiance does not seem to be a practical possibility. Acceptable propositions would have to be so general as not to be capable of supporting any concrete answer. One finds that at the great international conferences men fall into the realm of confusion as soon as they begin to speak of "spiritual values" even though up to that moment argument had been clear and to the point. It would seem that for many men the spiritual is a sphere where all is vague and people can

38

say anything at all, no matter what. For me, the sphere of the spiritual is as rigorous a discipline as that of any of the profane sciences. Theology is just as much a science as physics or linguistics. With it, as with them, only those who are competent can be expected to answer problems meaningfully.

This is where the function of religion in contemporary civilization is to be found. It is my belief that the only people who can contribute anything of value here are the authentic representatives of various religions. No one has found an ideology to replace that presented by the great historical religions. So even though the great world religions have problems to settle between them—and that is their business—they have today a common and indispensable function within the technical ordering of civilization. In performing this function they run up against politics, for Churches and religions are collective realities. While politics cannot touch the inner man, for this escapes completely from its competence, it can destroy the Churches. It can reach them because they are the collective expression of adoration. Not only can it do this, it does it.

The State can act as it does now in Russia : prevent children from entering church buildings; stop the teaching of catechism to groups; forbid even the use of buildings as churches—it can tear them down; prevent priests from exercising their functions—it can send them into concentration camps. Of course, there

39

will always be a number of religious souls, but the possibility of access to adoration for the poor, for children, for simple folk, and for families is practically destroyed. To the extent that the realization of their essential objects can be prevented by society, the survival of the Churches in a world of technology is a matter of politics.

However, one problem remains. We issue a challenge to politics and to the political societies of today when we tell them that it is vital for them that conditions in which prayer is possible should be maintained. They can make the same challenge to the Churches. In other words, the Churches justify their existence when they fulfil their function. If it is the function of the Churches to make prayer possible, the Churches justify themselves when through their efforts prayer becomes a reality. Churches which are but sociological remnants of sacral societies and in which mechanical rites continue to be performed; Churches which refuse to face the concrete realities of civilization; Churches enshrining sociological conditions which do not correspond to the claims of personality and within which religion is not personal and does not bear witness to a true interior life—the State can rightly consider these dead wood and legitimately cut them out. In other words, the Churches have to establish their claim to a place in the technological civilization of tomorrow. They have to show, through their

this is the problem w/ a purely functional critique — A speaker may speak the truth badly.

40

self-evident vitality, that there is indeed a function in the building of this civilization which they and they alone can fulfil.

This is the challenge that faces us. We are well aware that dialogue is two-sided. We have the right to ask for certain things from the earthly city, but the earthly city also has the right to ask certain things from us. Commenting on the request in the Lord's Prayer, "Forgive us our trespasses, as we forgive those who trespass against us," Pastor Dumas remarks "This is the dialogue between Church and State." The Church must pardon the State if it wants the State to pardon it. Men on both sides must recognize their faults. If we accuse the State and contemporary civilization of faults, let us also ask ourselves if they have not the right to reproach us for our faults. Have the Churches realized the importance of their mission or have they not rather in many cases remained fixed in attitudes that prevent them from being an effective force? We recognize here the same sort of dialogue as we have with some atheists. Here, as there, we find that religious men are reproached, not for being religious, but for not being religious enough; not for being Christian, but for not being truly so.

We are forced to conclude that, on the one hand, political society needs to create the sociological dimension necessary if prayer is to be the force in the world of tomorrow which will prevent that world from being inhuman; and, on the other hand, that sociological Christianity needs to transform itself in the Churches into that authentic life of prayer which is truly a personal meeting with the living God. This is the vital element which can justify the Church in asking the political society of tomorrow to reserve for it its proper place.

III

Christianity and Civilization

IT is vexing to have to discuss the question of Christian civilization, but nevertheless inevitable. Christian civilization is real enough, but its essence is hard to grasp. The term can be given many meanings, so that when I use the expression I cannot be sure that it means the same thing to all my readers. The word "civilization" may itself be taken in several senses. It can be taken to mean the totality of the technical and sociological arrangements which condition the collective life of mankind at a given point in time. It can be taken to mean the view of a particular human group on what man needs to realize his vocation. It is clear that "Christian civilization" takes on a different meaning according to whether one is referring to one or the other of these conceptions.

The ambiguity of Christian civilization is not in the words only. It lies in the essence of the concept, because it lies at the boundary of two worlds: that of the Church on the one side, with the supernatural purpose proper to it; and that of the earthly city on the other, with the human end proper to it. Christian

43

civilization, then, is characteristic of an essentially transitory world—one which is not that of the earthly cities, with their goods and gods, and which is not yet that of the celestial city, whose members are the saints and whose head is Christ. It is because it belongs to these two cities that Christian life in the world shows this fundamental ambiguity.

It would certainly be more convenient if Church and State were able to pursue their proper ends without reference to each other's activity. There are some thinkers today who hold that it is possible to separate Christianity from civilization, leaving responsibility for the first to a Church which would recognize that it had nothing to do with civilization, and responsibility for the second to a form of Marxism which would stop bothering about either religion or irreligion. Unfortunately, this *simpliste* solution is possible neither in fact nor in theory. The Church cannot disclaim any interest in temporal society, for that also is subject to the law of God of which the Church is the interpreter. So the Church has to drag the enormous weight of civilization along with it; and civilization has to carry the gaping wound of Christianity in its side; and this state of affairs must continue to the end of the world. It is of this that we have now to speak.

Our first need is to push unacceptable conceptions of Christian civilization to one side; we have to try to

44

keep clear of or to locate the ambiguities. The first of these, obviously, is the temptation to identify Christianity purely and simply with a Christian civilization. Here we are taking the word civilization at its highest meaning, as defining a set of values. We would call Christian a civilization whose institutions conformed to the divine law, still more one whose morals were penetrated with the Christian spirit. It is arguable whether such a civilization has ever existed. But even the fact that it has existed, might exist, or could exist, cannot justify equivocation by which it is identified with Christianity itself.

Nothing is more detestable than this degradation of Christianity. It is the "frightful illusion" of which Kierkegaard speaks. Christianity is not merely a theory about human life, even if it were the highest of such theories. It is a divine irruption which cuts through to the very seat of our wretchedness, prizing us loose from this civilization which can do no more than lighten our load, and brings us out on to a quite different level of existence. All civilization has to do with man in the flesh, the natural man, and with this world, the world of time and care. The essence of Christianity is the Spirit in the biblical sense of the word. It is the transfiguration of our woe. The final end which it sets before us is not the improvement of the earthly city, but the heavenly Jerusalem and its glory.

Nothing could be more degrading than to reduce

Christianity to an earthly ideal and make a philan-
thropist of Christ. We should not deceive ourselves,
however. Many are guilty of it who love Christ but
do not believe in him, for whom Christ is a prophet—
the greatest of the prophets, true, but only a prophet
and not the Word of God taking up our humanity in
his Incarnation, purifying it in the blood of his cross,
and taking it at his ascension into the House of his
Father.

It might well be that this way of seeing these events
could be a first step towards Christianity for the non-
Christian. There is no sense in it for a Christian. Our
alternative to Marxism is not a Christian civilization,
even as an ideal, which operates on the same level as
itself, but an affirmation of Christianity in all its fulness. It is not in the order of civilization that we have
first to look for the superiority of Christianity, but in
the fact that Christianity reaches to where civilization
cannot reach, to the root of man's wretchedness, to the
darkest places of his being—and that it alone brings
with it grace to heal.

The important events in Christianity are not those
which make up the history of civilizations. More important than the rise and fall of empires, the fame of
victories, the discoveries of scientists and scholars, the
masterpieces of art, are the Incarnation of the Word,
his Resurrection, the coming of the Holy Spirit, and the
mission of the Apostles, the conversion and the sancti-

fication of souls. Saints are more important to it than are geniuses or heroes. We shall say always with Pascal: "Jesus Christ, without possessions and producing nothing that human science could not compass, stands in his own order of sacredness. He made no invention, ruled no kingdom. He was humble, patient, holy before God, terrible to devils, entirely without sin."

This said and this first ambiguity removed, it remains true that there is such a thing as Christian civilization. There is historical evidence. For a large part of humanity Christianity has been and remains the religion which is a constitutive element of any complete civilization; and whatever may have been the reservations we have had to make just now, it remains true that it has exercised an influence both on institutions and on morals. There is a danger that the obvious defects of the civilizations which have been called Christian may blind us to this fact. They must not be allowed to do so. Christianity has done much to heighten respect for the human person, to better the condition of women, to emphasize the brotherhood which exists between men of all races.

But there is also a permanent reality in Christian civilization. That the end proper to Christianity relates to the highest destiny of mankind has been insisted on enough to allow us to recall that it is not for this reason uninterested in men's earthly destinies. This is true in a double sense. On the one hand, the earthly city is subject to the Law of God, not, it is true, in its particular applications, but in the principles which govern them. The Church has always asserted its right and duty to intervene in this domain, basing its claim to do so on the fact that it has the care of the Natural Law. (We would prefer to call this the divine law, for it is from God that it acquires its whole authority in the eyes of the Christian.)

However, this view is only partial. To the extent that institutions are in the last resort no more than expressions of human relationships, normally they reflect the spirit which rules those relationships. It is to be expected that the transformation which the Gospel spirit brings to human relationships should manifest itself at the institutional level. This is particularly evident as regards the institution of the family. Of course, this influence is always limited and always struggling, sharing as it must in the ambiguousness of Christian civilization; but that there is an influence cannot be denied. The tragedy is not that Christians have tried to penetrate civilization with the spirit of the Gospel, but that they have not done it sufficiently.

Besides, the Church cannot fail to have an interest in civilization to the extent that the city of this world must subordinate itself to the city of eternity. The Church has been given by God himself the task of leading men to this heavenly city, and has therefore the

48

right to ask of the earthly city that it put no obstacle in the way. Although Christianity cannot be affected by any sociological conditions and can spring up under any sort of circumstance, it remains true that a Christian people cannot exist without a milieu to sustain it. It cannot survive in a world where the institutions are morally perverse or ideologically misconceived. In this sense, Christianity ought for the sake of its own final end to seek to influence the institutions of the earthly city.

However, it is necessary to add that although it is legitimate to speak of Christian civilization, it is dangerous to make a myth out of it and to let it be believed that the kingdom of God is a possibility on earth. For although civilization may not necessarily be impure, it is of necessity narrow and of short duration. It is a world of righteousness which is not that of the Beatitudes, of a knowledge which is not Christ's knowledge; it is a world whose forces can be tamed but never finally subdued, and whose successes are precarious and of small extent. This should not surprise us, for we know that the kingdom of God is not of this world—or rather, that in so far as it does exist in this world it exists only in the hearts of the saints, hidden now but to be made manifest in the fulness of time.

It is to be noted also that Christian civilization is not without temptation for Christians. So long as they are persecuted by the powers of this world, they have no difficulty in holding fast to a hope that goes beyond the earthly city. Once let them become masters of the city and they stand in danger of getting bogged down in it. It is never entirely without risk for men to handle money or to be active in politics. How many there are who have undertaken such activities with the best intentions and been trapped! The greatest danger for the Christian does not come from persecution but from worldliness. The drama of Christian civilization lies in the fact that engagement in temporal affairs is at one and the same time a duty and a temptation. There must be a tension between care for the last things, judgement, hell, and heaven, and solicitude for the advance of civilization; and there is a danger that this will be allowed to slacken and the right articulation of one with the other go undiscovered.

This brings us to a new aspect of the ambiguity in Christian civilization, to an explanation of why it is that the Christians who are most irritated by the term are often those most engaged in temporal affairs. This points to a feeling of unease. However, such uneasiness does not arise out of Christian civilization as such, but from our civilization in so far as it is styled Christian. It is not at all clear how far the present state of affairs has any right to be called Christian, and it is by no means easy to clarify the ambiguity.

The view of some people is that there was a truly Christian civilization in the Middle Ages and that this continued into the seventeenth century, but was then undermined by the Renaissance. For those people, we are now living in a period of decadence and witnessing the dissolution of western Christian civilization.

An exactly opposite point of view has been defended by the Austrian writer Friedrich Heer. He argues that the medieval institutions which formed the backbone of that civilization had not been truly christianized. The right of ownership, in particular, had remained the *jus utendi et abutendi* of the Romans and had not been changed to take account of the Judeo-Christian principle that the purpose for which goods exist is more important than their ownership. In the same way, the modern awakening of nationalist passions shows how little such feelings had been affected by the unity of Christendom. Heer concludes that "there has never been in Europe in any true sense a Christianity which was widespread, living, and fruitful. . . ." For him, Christian civilization belongs more to the future than to the past.

Both of these points of view are doubtless mistaken. Institutions evolve over time, being the expression of new economic, political, and social situations. As Mounier remarked, Christianity does not give rise to institutions directly. It works alongside those which exist, purifying them of their excesses and bringing them into conformity with the demands of the spirit. It was in this way that it acted on slavery, not con-

51

demning it as such but creating a spirit which rendered its continuance impossible. The work is unceasing, and has always to be begun anew as conditions change. In this sense there is a fundamental ambiguity in Christian civilization, and we have not to be scandalized that it should exist in ours.

But there is another ambiguity—not this time inescapable—which causes us trouble. It is true that the Christian civilization which is ours is heir to authentic Christian values. This is forgotten by those who claim that the structure of the western civilization of today is fundamentally bad and ought to be replaced by another which would truly permit Christianity to flourish. Such a view is a dangerous illusion, for it fails to value properly the really authentic civilization that exists in family life, in personal rights, and in the cultural foundations of the society in which we live. It would be frivolous of those who are its beneficiaries and heirs to see only its failures and to hold it cheap.

However, it is also true that this civilization is not truly Christian, for it is not faithful to its own principles. This explains our repugnance to calling it Christian, for we find the term dreadfully pharisaical. We are easily led to hold our civilization cheap, not because we scorn Christian civilization, but because we feel that the high idea we had of it has been betrayed; and our resentment leads us to prefer a civilization which is in no way Christian to one which misrepresents

Christianity. May it not be that the hostility which some Christians today show to the idea of a Christian civilization is the expression of a disappointed love?

The fact remains that such a position is dangerous even though some people find its radicalism appealing. The influence of Christianity on civilization has never been as great as could have been desired, and nothing therefore could be more dangerous or misguided than to spurn all that has come down from Christian times. It is true that in some of its forms this heritage could appear to be responsible for outmoded cultural or social dispositions, but beyond these external features there are certain human values of permanent importance which have been acquired. These must not be rejected. They must be expressed in forms more adapted to the present time. It is perfectly possible to bring a country from a Christian civilization of the traditional type to one that is refashioned without passing through a bout of dechristianization.

There, after all, lies the real problem. What matters is not to cling to historical forms for their own sake, but to meet fully a requirement springing from the very essence of Christianity. To this requirement there are two sides. There is first of all the expression of the fact that Christ has come to save all that has been made. Redemption is concerned with all creation. It leads it to its goal. But civilization is part of the order of creation, being the expression of man's deployment

53

of his forces as he realizes his vocation to complete the world through his intelligence and work. The civilizations of history are simply different aspects of this fundamental civilization.

Christianity is not bound up with any particular civilization, whether in time or place. It is of the essence of Christianity, on the other hand, to come to the rescue of all that has been created, and hence of the work and effort of mankind. In this sense, civilization has need of Christianity, even in its own order, being by man's sin shut off from the fulness of its own development, even on the natural plane. It is sick and needs to be healed, like all things that pertain to man in his wounded state. Indeed, one of the characteristics of our own civilization is a consciousness of the dangers brought to humanity by human progress itself in so far as that progress is not freed from the forces of darkness, from the will to dominate or the passion to seize and hold, from all that betrays it and turns it away from its purpose.

On the other hand, Christianity too has need of civilization. Christianity must take up and consecrate all that has to do with man. Therefore it must not ignore that side of human reality which concerns work. It is not tied to the culture of any particular place, nor to that of any particular time. Rather, it is bound to all. The modern world is no exception. This, too, God has given to Christianity for it to consecrate, and it would be shuffling out of its responsibilities if it refused to face the task. It is true that industrial civilization began outside Christianity; but it is true also that it cannot come to fruition except with the aid of Christianity. It is the material on which Christianity has to work.

I have no liking for Christians who will not touch the facts of human existence for fear of soiling their hands. The Christians who struggle to make Christianity effective in the world, even at the cost of painful blows, those I admire. I love that Church which plunges into the thickets of human history and is not afraid of compromising itself by getting mixed up with men's affairs, with their political conflicts and their cultural disputes. I love that Church because it loves men and therefore goes out to look for them wherever they are. And I love best of all that Church which is mud-splashed from history because it has played its part in history, that Church of the poor which is denounced for its weaknesses by pharisees whose hands are clean but who can point to no single person they have saved.

mud-splashed

IV

Technology and Man

WE have found that it is not possible to keep Christianity and civilization apart. Christ comes to retake possession of the full nature of man and we cannot exclude what is on the level of earthly existence. On the one hand, Christianity must take to itself all man's values; while, on the other, man cannot fulfil himself except through Christianity. Within this ultimate perspective there are problems to be dealt with at several different levels. The world of technology itself brings dangers for men; and there is the risk of man's trying to make himself whole without God. Beside all this, the problem of religious man is not the same as the problem of Christian revelation.

These different levels, on which we have now to operate, cannot be completely separated from one another, but it is none the less important to distinguish clearly between them. They can be ranged in a sort of ecumenical hierarchy: the first problem affecting all men; the second affecting all religious men; the third affecting all Christians. We shall begin with that which deals with all mankind face to face with technological civilization.

The question set by technical progress and its applications is not simply a moral problem. It goes far beyond that. In the last resort it involves a view of the nature and significance of man within a wider and more comprehensive vision. It is clear from the outset that we have to look at technology in itself from a positive point of view. It would be absurd to look upon it as an evil thing. The few thinkers who argue that it is operate on a plane of unreality, and are without interest for this enquiry. It is my view, and here I speak as a theologian, that if we place ourselves in the perspective of the Bible, which is that also of Christianity, we must take a positive view of technical progress. From the theoretical point of view we have no reason whatsoever for being suspicious of it.

I will go further, and add that we ought to bear witness to all the benefits we owe to technical progress. That there is a debit side is true, and we shall come to it; but the credit side is enormous in extent, and cannot but arouse in us an immense gratitude to science. When I think of all the suffering which medical and surgical developments now prevent, I have the impression that there is in humanity today, I will not say happiness, but a possibility of happiness, or at least of conditions making for happiness, if only men can learn to utilize them. Such possibilities were out of reach in those tragic times when infantile mortality was high and cholera and the plague could destroy civilizations just as effectively as could now the atomic bomb. We have no apprehension of such scourges today. Then again, just at the time when fears might begin to be felt about the exhaustion of the earth's resources, hope comes from the exploration of the riches of the universe. Atomic energy arrives just when there are fears for the sufficiency of coal and oil reserves. Indeed, it seems to us that the progress of science is reaching a quite extraordinary stage.

It is of course difficult to be clear about science and technology, because they can be put to such opposing uses. The problem which science thus poses has always existed, but it is today presented to us in a much more acute manner because of the extraordinarily powerful techniques made available by modern technology. A problem not different in kind from that which men faced in the past has become so much greater quantitatively as to be something new. All the same, it is necessary to put it at its true level, which is not that of technology itself but of the place which science and technology have taken in the scheme of values that constitutes a thoroughgoing humanism. On the one hand, science has held itself to be capable of explaining all that could be known, scientific methods being thought apt to solve every problem posed by human

58

existence. On the other hand, at the level of applied science, the dream of freeing man from all his ills, a sort of salvation of mankind by technology, has come to take the place of religious salvation. The new dogma flourished in the nineteenth century and has lived into the twentieth. It is not long since a reputable philosopher argued in a published work that every ill that threatened man would be conquered by the progress of science.

The essential mischief of contemporary science lies in this kind of myth, that science or technology is capable of resolving the fundamental problems of mankind. It has led to a loss of balance in men's thinking today. Physical sciences are being pursued with extraordinary vigour, while other disciplines, just as fundamental and just as scientific, such as ethics, metaphysics, and theology, are strangely and tragically put to one side. We shall say more of this presently. Meantime, modern science leads us on a false trail in the sense that when it is examining critically the answers it itself obtains, it imagines that it is questioning those on which the essential values of existence are founded.

Today, however, a movement against this trend begins to make itself felt, and the possibilities opened up by the new developments in technology have brought an awakening in two directions.

First, men are becoming aware of the responsibility

of the expert, and conscious that scientific research cannot be dissociated from morality. A fundamental question is posed here, and while I do not claim to be able here and now to give a quick answer to it, I can at least point to its existence. Oppenheimer gives outstanding witness in our time to the moral anguish of a great scholar in face of the dangers that science and its development can create for mankind. He testifies to an awakening in scientific circles to moral problems and to a feeling that science is not enough of itself to resolve them. It seems to me that we are seeing the creation of a new type of man, the responsible man of science. It seems to me also that this development of a sense of responsibility and this preoccupation with ethics among scientists comes at a time when among those engaged in literary pursuits there is a decline which is in many respects dreadfully disquieting. One of the grounds for my optimism is the human development of those engaged in scientific research and the way in which they feel the need to go beyond and complete their scientific formation with a study of ethics and metaphysics. Through physics we shall eventually come back to metaphysics, for the one is not complete without the other.

In the second place, side by side with this awakening to responsibility is a consciousness of a lack of balance in modern man, an apprehension that some human values appear to have been insufficiently cared for. The nostalgia for oriental wisdom which is found in some circles is a kind of defensive reaction to this loss. It can be asked whether, from some interior urge rather than external moral command, men will not be moved to a rediscovery of whole realms of reality which have been ignored by technological culture, but which have not for that reason ceased to exist. It can be asked, too, whether the investigation of man as a moral being will not be one of the great fields of research in the future, after so long a period of tragic neglect. It is through the almost inherent development of humanity in its growth that certain values can thus be rediscovered.

The question, then, with which we are faced today is what place to give to technology within a more complete vision of the nature of man. To have true meaning, it must be subordinated to the highest ends of mankind. The progress that has been made brings us sharply up against this, and makes us aware of situations with which technology is incapable of dealing. These are problems which primarily concern the integrity of the human person, and here it is questions of biology that are of outstanding importance. Biology touches two of the fundamental realities of human existence, perhaps the only two that are really fundamental: love and death. As biology progresses in its study of the way in which life is transmitted, it makes us aware that there is in sex something which goes

61

beyond biology; it encounters love. When biology is put to uses which threaten interpersonal relations that go beyond biology: in other words, when it threatens to undermine that personal love which binds a man and a woman and that climate of love in which alone a child can become a balanced personality, it touches the very essence of humanity.

Biology has to deal also with death. There is the problem of knowing up to just what point life should be prolonged; and there is the challenge of death, which is for many men the occasion of being really themselves, for perhaps the first time, and of making a really decisive choice. In the use to which they are put, the forces made available by technology must respect those facts of humanity which show the transcendence of the human person over all material circumstances. It is this which obliges us to distinguish between the forces that affect man and man himself, who, although he is subject to them, yet belongs to quite a different order.

We are not merely playing with words. We are conducting a serious enquiry, and it is clear that we ought to be considering some concrete solutions towards which we can move in the immediate future. Some can be at once dismissed as incomplete or misleading. There is, for example, the notion that scientific discovery could be kept more or less secret in a world where publicity has already become a matter of necessity. It it said of Leonardo da Vinci that he kept to himself the secret of the submarine, fearing that others would not share his view that it was a dastardly act to fire on another vessel when one's own was invisible. It would be impossible for him to conceal his invention today. In the same way, it is not possible to control the technological applications of theoretical advances. This is not to say that there are not real problems here, for technological procedures take different directions.

One possibility for the future is that the great pioneers of the technological world of tomorrow will take a collective stand on grounds of conscience, and, pushing aside the claims of business and political power, bear witness to a new world ethic and make themselves as a group masters of the discoveries of which they are themselves the authors. It would seem that we have the right to expect this of them, even though political divisions in the world make such a universal college of scholars a very difficult thing to achieve.

An essential part of the problem is that today science is no longer a matter of individual intuition. The responsibility of an individual for the next step forward in a seemingly inexorable process is to some extent diminished. If one man does not make the discovery, another will. This consideration raises the question whether in fact the problem has not ceased to be a matter for the conscience of the individual researcher but rather one raised at the collective level, be it from the point of view of science or morality. It does appear that there is today a sort of collective conscience, that is to say, a feeling for certain fundamental values, such as respect for human dignity and freedom. It is true that this can be overthrown on occasion by political forces, but it does nevertheless seem to be something real and powerful on which we can count to regulate and correct technological progress and make it serve the true good of humanity. Progress at this level would consist in a discovery of those common values which would allow the future of mankind to be seen as a function of a certain conception of the nature of man.

These values of the collective conscience have a real influence on the development of humanity, but the element of vitality and power also plays a part. It would be an illusion, for example, to believe that the forces of nationalism are destined to diminish. Quite the contrary. The world of today shows an even greater consciousness than ever of nationality, and this is a creative and constructive element of the humanity of tomorrow. The world is not moulded only by techniques, nor is it the product only of ideas. There is a part also for those vital forces which spring from the peoples themselves. The problem is how to make these different components converge. So far as I am concerned—and this is one of the points on which I have just been insisting—it would be a mistake to trace everything back to the problems of technology. That is only one aspect of the vital forces in the world. Is it not remarkable how, just when it might be thought that the world could be unified through technology, the way to unity is blocked by the awakening of new nationalisms? It seems to me that these forces are a healthy protection for humanity against the threat of a technological civilization which could lead mankind to a collective uniformity, where originality and the values of feeling and imagination which express the spirit of peoples could be thrown away. Once again I come back to the idea that what is important is to create a humanism in which diverse constitutive forces would be respected.

Finally, technological progress should not make us overestimate the novelty of modern man. Men are subject to new forces, of which technology itself is the outstanding example. But this is all that is new. Man himself as a person, in his spiritual being, his freedom and his intelligence, does not seem to me to be in any way new at all. We are not more intelligent than were Plato and Aristotle. We have new means at our disposal; but I do not see that man has changed one whit in his own nature.

It is not human values themselves which are set vibrating by the shock of modern technology, but the scientific matrix in which they are embedded. It is this matrix which we must allow to be broken up. It is this of which we must be rid if we are to confront all the circumstances of modern science while continuing to hold that man has an intellect capable of reaching metaphysical as well as scientific truth.

I will take the example of immortality. This presents us with an interesting problem that will help us to set out the different levels of discourse.

First we have the problem thrown up by biological technique, the problem of a-mortality, the greater or lesser lengthening of the span of life. The prolongation of biological existence raises no difficulty in itself. At the same time, it must be said that there seems to be something contradictory in the idea of an indefinitely prolonged biological existence, for it is of the essence of such existence to grow to fulness of being and then to decline. Besides, the indefinite prolongation of biological existence would be something dreadfully disappointing.

On the other side there is the metaphysical problem of immortality, the problem posed by Plato. I think that metaphysics can arrive with certainty at the proposition that there is in man a principle going beyond biology, which certainly is tied up with biology, but which can in no way be reduced to biology. It must not be forgotten that this metaphysical belief in the immortality of the soul is not merely the characteristic of the higher civilizations, but has been held by all mankind. If there is one common element in the whole of human history, it is precisely the certitude that those whom we call the dead are living, and that life cannot simply be blotted out, so that it becomes essential to have communication and communion with those who are no more. In contemporary terms, the metaphysical problem does not so much concern one's own death as what Gabriel Marcel calls "the death of the loved one"; that is to say, we have to do with the fact that love defies biological death. This sort of certainty is of a quite different order from anything to which technology can attain, and human intelligence has the right to hold by it.

The fact of the matter is that technological man is being driven by the facts themselves to rediscover the other aspects of his humanism which he had abandoned. The pressure does not come from without, but from within himself. The values are not rediscovered as a heritage from the past; nor in a form which in no way recalls the past; but as just what they are : unvarying and fundamental characteristics of the human person. At the root of the crisis we have been examining there lies this subtle play between ever-changing technology and a human personality which keeps its character unchanged. This interplay makes us aware of the predominance of the technological element, but it shows us also how this very element leads, by a sort of necessary correlation, to the rediscovery of the other elements. The meaning of the clash between responsibility and technology is found in this, that it is technology itself which leads us today to a rediscovery of the permanent values of a complete humanism.

V

Art, Technology and the Sacred

THE principal characteristic of the world of today is the development of scientific thinking and technological organization. It is both admirable and irreversible. It overthrows barriers and widens horizons, but it also awakens a new consciousness of man that is more creative, more universal, and more organized. Science as such does not constitute this consciousness; it calls out for it. There is an immense appeal going up from this universe. It is for others—philosophers, writers, artists—to provide for it the awareness it cannot be denied. There is undoubtedly a lack of synchronization between the condition of the technical infrastructure and that of the human superstructure. Philosophy, literature, and art express not so much a human perception of this new world as the dismay of old-fashioned man faced with a world to which he is not attuned. Hence the element of despair, the sense of absurdity, the protest and the revolt.

There is another tendency also, one which does nothing to meet the problem. This is the movement which seeks to make modern art only a reflection of technology. As Francine Virduzzo said recently: "A work of art has an authenticity which can never be reduced to a mere phenomenon of scientific application or scientific unfolding. While the artist should not stand aside from his own time, neither should he reduce himself to a merely parascientific dimension. In other words, for the artist to make a work of art it is not enough for him to participate in the scientific and humanist evolution of his universe. A work of art, whether it be industrial or handicraft, by implication goes beyond the technical fact." That seems to me to be well said. The artist has to be a man of his time and must therefore be today in some sort a technologist. He must do more than hold a mirror to technology; he must give it meaning. The artists of today lack ambition. They allow technology to dazzle and enslave them.

What science asks of them is something more than a bored commentary on its progress. Science opens out upon the sacred, in the confrontation between the atom and world suicide, between the physician and death, between eugenics and love; but if it is to discover the sacred, science must have a means of expression. This is where art is to find its role. It must play upon the world of technology, which is like a muffled drum, and enable it to find its voice.

My contention that the role is one of mediation calls

for some explanation. The problem is to find a way of expressing sacred things which will correspond to the development of science and technology. The difficulty lies in bringing together the two worlds of science and technology on the one side and the world of sacred things on the other. Our tragedy today is that the bridges between them have been cut. A means of presenting one to the other is lacking; there is no imagery which can serve this role. What I am saying is that while science cannot give a picture of itself, the world of the sacred lays emphasis on imagery. Art can place itself at this frontier. While the artist as such is neither physicist nor metaphysicist, without him physics cannot lead to metaphysics.

This is the problem that is posed by technological civilization. Before the age of technology civilization was essentially religious. In the modern world this element has been removed by technology even more perhaps than by science. Man has moved from contemplation to production. He lives surrounded by the products of his inventiveness and skill, and sees in them the image of his own greatness. The heavens may bear witness to God's glory, but machines bear witness to the glory of man. There is a movement in the art of today which reflects this concentration of interest upon the making of things. Art is wedded to technical change; it elucidates its lines and prefigures its results. It ceases to be a way to knowledge and becomes a principle of production. In this way it serves to affirm man's power over his world, and the artist becomes a sharer in the excitements of the technical revolution. All of this corresponds with an area in which man is sovereign, and the question is to know whether art ought to be enclosed within it or to move beyond it. It must in any case enter into it. That in itself takes away any sacral value, at least in the first instance.

Can this be taken to be the definitive position? Here we touch on a point which is essential to the actual problem: the elimination of myths. Art comes directly into the question. Let us consider how the matter arises. For those who are impressed with the importance of technology it becomes necessary to accept a separation between the sacred and the natural. Henceforth, nature must be thought of as completely secularized and demythologized. It is no longer a sign of the divine, but belongs entirely to man's domain. The sacred is pushed away into a quite different universe, one that is without contact with the world of nature. There must be complete breakaway if it is to be reached. It belongs to the realm of pure faith. This is the position of Bultmann and Tillich.

This reaction is born of a feeling of panic which in its turn is caused by the way in which faith has become tied to an outworn view of the world. That this has happened is no reason for holding that faith should be connected with no world view at all. If faith were to be cut off in this way from human experience, it would itself become inaccessible. Very few people could live in so rarefied an atmosphere. Plato's vision of mankind as divided between a few philosophers and a mass of workers would become reality. Nothing could be further from Christianity than this theory of an élite. Even so, there is a danger that such a division may come to pass. If we are not careful, mankind tomorrow will consist of a few monastic communities dedicated to pure contemplation, standing apart from an immense mass of atheists consecrated to the production of material goods. Such a prospect fills me with horror. If we wish to avoid it we must have imagery.

This crisis came upon us three hundred years ago, with Galileo and Pascal. Perhaps Teilhard has begun the movement that will resolve it. For Pascal, as for Jansenism, there is a conflict, a ripping apart, an abyss between an interior experience which has no outside evidence of its existence and a cold world which contradicts it. There is a tragic coexistence of a deaf world from which God is absent and a heart which is aware of God. The evidence of the heart is passionately preferred to the denials of the world. But such evidence, being purely subjective and incommunicable, is inaccessible to the mass of men, whose destiny it is to be involved in affairs of the natural order. The world must speak of God; otherwise, man can normally have no access to him.

Is it really true that the world is silent? Has the world ever been questioned? How can it speak if it has no language? To give it a language is the task of art.

In this task there are two stages: first, of representation, then of orientation. The world of science is inaccessible to the majority of men because it is, as it were, dumb. This being so, men believe themselves to be in a world which has in fact already passed away. The task that falls to art is to understand and express on a human scale what the universe of modern science really is, and in this way to make the world meaningful. A beginning has been made, but the completion of the task will be a long and wearying job. The very stuff of the universe must, as it were, be seized at the level both of the infinitely great and the infinitely small. This is what abstract painting tries to do when it gets away from purely subjective experience and tries to express the elements of reality.

The first thing that art needs to do is to go to school in the world of science. It must listen before it can explain. It must accept strict discipline. It is only in so far as reality is accepted that meanings can be elucidated and put into a language that the world can be made to speak. Rilke has likened the poet to a man in

74

the dark, alone, like a vein of ore. There must be nothing here of the arbitrary. It is the most humble and laborious efforts that are today the most truly authentic. Men must not fall victim to the merely facile, to demagogy, to counterfeits of the sacred.

These temptations do exist. So great is the need of our world for mystery that some men are only too ready to provide cheap imitations of it. There is an attraction in the fantastic and in some types of surrealism. It is possible to call up fleeting visions as entrancing as opium dreams, but which leave only a taste of ashes behind them. Magicians are ready to profit from the boredom of our technological civilization and to offer us quack remedies for it. But the delusions they offer provide no real escape. Man's sickness remains.

It is to the real world that a voice must be given; it is only from reality that the truly sacred emerges, like sap in a vigorous tree. The world of modern science can become hierophantic in a higher degree than could the pretechnical civilizations, which now appear to us as singularly cramped and limited. Modern science opens up the immense field of inter-stellar space. It conquers matter, looks into its heart, reaches at its origin to the instability of the primal elements, and comes by way of the infinitely small to that which is symbolic of the spiritual. In the depths of time it finds a dimension unknown to the ancients, an ordered movement or evolution, which is like an image of the infinite in living action and fully master of itself.

We come now to orientation. The picture of the world which science gives us is two-dimensional. It does not show us man in depth. When the background elements have been analysed it is necessary to proceed to the human dimension properly so called, both in its infinite complexity as portrayed by Teilhard de Chardin and its depth as shown by Tillich. It is in this that art triumphs over science, it is here that its worth appears. Area becomes volume, sunk in an unknown world, and art expresses this dimension. This is particularly true of the study of the human body, which takes on artistic value when it ceases to be merely an object and becomes a mystery which escapes our grasp. That is why eroticism so quickly becomes boring. It seeks to reduce the body to a machine, but in so doing it takes away that dimension of the sacramental or the sacrilegious, of heaven or of hell, which gives it its real fascination.

Thus, the general picture of the universe which art succeeds in giving is a better likeness than the picture given by science. Indeed, it would be true to say that science does not give any picture of the universe at all. Modern science is becoming more and more aware that all it can express are relations of one thing to another. The world of science has no centre; and man feels himself lost, disorientated in such a world. It is here that the dignity of art becomes apparent. Taking the findings of science as a starting-point, it organizes the universe into a cosmos, giving it order. This order is of a higher level than that of science because it takes more completely into account the fulness of reality. It allows man to find his bearings and rid himself of the feeling that he is astray. It gives him landmarks.

The constitution of a sacred cosmos is one of art's essential tasks and could be said to be a never-ending one. From this point of view, those who opposed Galileo were in the right of it within their own frame of reference. Their universe was true enough. Their mistake lay in thinking that their universe was also the universe of science. It was not this, but a representation of the sacral universe and of man's place therein. This sacral cosmos corresponds to that of the Hindu *mandir* (temples) with their successive courts leading up to the sanctuary; to that of the Persian gardens with their concentric terraces; to that of the Byzantine churches, the cupolas of which are as microcosms; to that of the baroque churches or of the paintings of Altdorfer, with their skies opened up to show the Holy Trinity above the angelic choirs.

Rilke was not mistaken when he identified as one the sphere of the angels and the sphere of all that is beautiful. "For the beautiful is nothing but the first degree of the terrible." The world of beauty is the world of intermediary hierarchies which are irradiated with the glory that cascades down from the Trinity even into the formless opacity of matter. The beautiful is the world of forms between that which is above form, being the sphere of God, and that which has no form at all, being mere matter. The modern world shuts out that intermediate order. It recognizes nothing between scientific thinking and mystical possession, and in so doing denies completely the sphere which it is the function of art to reconstitute by giving back to the universe its depths.

Until now we have left aside one aspect of the technological civilization of today, the raising of human standards. This is more a matter of technology than of science in itself, and that for several reasons. The first is that improvements in material conditions of life reflect back necessarily on to social organization, and lead to a greater consciousness of the personal dignity of men in all walks of life. Secondly, as we have already seen, technology makes man conscious of his power and develops a sense of his standing and importance. Lastly, technological civilization awakens in mankind a consciousness of unity and solidarity, both in the dangers which threaten and in the opportunities which are opened up.

Thence arises a question. It is certain, let us remind ourselves, that the way in which technological man is part of a self-centred collectivity seems at first to shut him off from sacred things. In so far as men feel themselves to be strong, they feel that much less need of help. In so far as they see themselves as more to be admired, they are that much less inclined to admire anything greater than themselves. From some points of view man grows into a screen which shuts off the sight of God, or a lens which concentrates attention and admiration upon himself. On the other hand, when man is confronted with this technological position, he sees more clearly how limited is the help technology can give him. It leaves him unprovided for in precisely those situations which have the most importance for him.

Such situations must be seen to have a meaning and importance which go beyond themselves. Here again art has an essential part to play. It is clear that the modern cinema of Bergmann or Bunuel goes far beyond mere description. It confronts man continually with extreme cases of loneliness, captivity, and despair. That is to say, it shows men in situations which are meaningful because they point a lesson. Even where it does not show forth a meaning, and rests ambiguous, it none the less creates a world of free association.

It is a remarkable discovery that the meanings elucidated by contemporary art lead back to precisely those situations which underlie the symbolism of the Bible. The situation of Israel in its escape from Egypt, and that of those who are freed by baptism on Easter day, are situations of captivity and liberation. The drama of the alliance between Yahweh and Israel is described in the Bible in terms borrowed from human love—fidelity and unfaithfulness. The problem of the apparent meaninglessness of suffering is the theme of the Book of Job, while the passion of the search for justice fills the works of the prophets. So true is all this that modern art often makes reference to biblical themes, even when it empties them of all sacred content.

With that last admission we are able to answer a possible objection. To say that art enables us to go beyond the world of technology into the world of man is not necessarily the same thing as to say that it brings us also to the world of sacred things. It can remain at a purely human level. The point is that even at the human level we see art becoming a principle of release in bringing out the significant force of the human situation. By this I mean that we can find in it at all levels that kind of dynamism which makes it an excellent medium for explaining one side to the other. This dynamism can be interpreted in different ways, and I do not say that art in itself offers a meaning. Rather, by its means actual realities can be given a meaning, and the sacred be thereby provided with a language.

Thus, art and the sacred have a common destiny. Without art, the sacred cannot reach out to the mass of men. Without the sacred, art is swallowed up by technology. Together, they can give a reply to the cry put up by the world of technology when it asks for a vision that shall lead to a communion, a unity of spirit, a civilization. Technology gives this civilization the infrastructure on which the city has to be built and the homes of men and the House of God to rest. It is a magnificent task which restores to art its human function. This is what art has to understand.

VI

Religion and Revelation

MEN of all religions realize that they have today a common responsibility before all that endangers the place of God in the civilization of tomorrow. This consideration suggests that we should reflect on the nature of the non-Christian religions and on their relationship to the Christian revelation. Indeed, it is only if we start from a clearly defined position in this matter that we can avoid, on the one hand, syncretism, which assimilates Christianity to religion in general, even though it be regarded as by far the best of all religions; and, on the other, sectarianism, which disregards the positive content of the non-Christian religions. This question is of importance today, whether it be for the way in which the Christian message is to be presented, or the possibilities of dialogue and co-operation with non-Christians, or the appreciation of the pagan elements in Christianity.

I shall confine my remarks to the case presented by the pagan religions, which means those which exist outside the historic revelation. Thus, I leave to one side the question of Judaism, this being a quite special field of enquiry. Islam, also, I put aside, for it contains elements borrowed from both Judaism and Christianity. I ignore also the non-religious world which is sometimes mistakenly termed pagan. The pagan is essentially a religious man, and nothing is more contrary to paganism than godlessness.

That which finds expression in the diversity of religions is a quality of human nature. Religious activity is a constitutive part of man. That this is so is proved by history, by psychology, and by philosophy. For the ethnologist, tools and worship are signs that men are present. The psychologist also finds in the depths of the human personality something which cannot be reduced to any other sphere of experience. This is even more true for the philosopher, for whom authentic humanism is found where man displays the three sides of his nature: mastery over the universe by technology, communion with others through love, and conversion to God in adoration.

From this point of view, religion does not refer solely to another world. Religious experience is a constitutive element of this world. It is an aberration on the part of modern laicism to imagine that humanism can exist apart from religion. A world without God is an inhuman world. God is a party to civilization. This is true, of course, at the level of the individual, for whom the love of God is a condition of his fulfilment and happiness. But it is true also at the level of the community. Religious activity forms part of the temporal common good; and this is true whatever form religious experience may take.

Very many attempts have been made to explain religious experience away. There have been cosmological explanations—that the mystery of nature is only that which is as yet unexplained; psychological—that religion is only a sublimation of instinct, particularly of the sexual instinct; and sociological—transcendency merely expresses the submission of the individual to the family or the national group. All of these observations start from well founded facts, but all misinterpret the facts. They confuse the signs of the sacred with its substance.

After all, it is the peculiar quality of religions to understand the signs by which the divine presence is revealed. These signs are of different orders. They can be cosmological phenomena : the starry sky; a thunderstorm; the enduring, unchanging, majestic mountains; the snake, still water, and the moon, suggesting fertility; all these are signs in which men throughout history have seen evidence of a divine presence.

Still more is it through human gestures that the presence of what is holy can be perceived. One of the most fundamental characteristics of all religions is the consecration of the important events in life. The birth of a child, its entry into adolescence, marriage, and death are always the occasion of ceremonial. There is a liturgical cycle to mark the seasonal rhythm of work. Human rites are copied from those performed by the gods in the world of the ideal. Rite and myth are expressions of a fundamental experience by which man reaches out to a world beyond his ken.

Positivist explanations of religion are at fault, therefore, when they try to turn the outward sign of religion into the substance of it. As Eliade and Van der Leeuw rightly perceived, it was not the sun we see that the disciples of Mithras adored, but in it the beneficent power which gives light and life. And although, as Lévi-Strauss saw, religion expresses itself in social structures, it is not therefore to be identified with them. Rather, it is in fundamental human relationships that man is reunited to a reality which is not his to possess but which brings him into contact with the unattainable.

Lastly, it is within himself, in his experience both of his weakness and his immense strength, that man perceives the presence of something divine, something which is in him and works through him, yet is not part of him. He finds it in the motions of his conscience, which compel him to recognize the utter incompatibility of good and evil; in the light of his reason, which reveals to him the presence of a truth living at the very centre of his being; in the calls of a love which drives him to go far beyond all that is finite to seek that

Good from which all goodness receives its virtue. And sometimes, searching his own heart, he finds to his surprise the reflection there of a light that comes from elsewhere.

This world of religion is one of the privileged sectors of human experience. Humanity may be enriched by scientific discoveries and social advances, but its inmost being can never be so fully expressed as it is in religion. The great religions of history are expressions of the religious drive in mankind. Though they are many, yet are they one. All are expressions of the same level of experience. Each in its own way, they make visible to us the way in which men have recognized God's presence in the world and have sought him beyond its confines.

Even so, it is of their nature to differ from one another. Each expresses the religious genius of a people; and there is nothing more characteristic of a people than its religion. From this point of view the old tag *"Cujus regio, ejus religio"* is perfectly true. The religion of a people is so much a part of its heritage that a man could no more betray his religion than betray his race. And indeed it is absurd to change a religion when that religion is the form in which the religious genius of a people finds expression. Religions are part of the richness of creation, and one of its most remarkable aspects. How could Christianity destroy them, when its mission is not to destroy but to fulfil, when it comes to save all that has been created?

When we look at the matter in this way, we see that nothing could be more false than to make of Christianity the religion of the West. Christianity is of quite a different order. There was at one time a religion of the West, the paganism of antiquity, Greek or Roman, Celtic or Teutonic. That religion was the equivalent of Hinduism or Taoism, of animism or the American religions. Sankara can be compared to Plotinus, and Marcus Aurelius to Confucius. This western paganism was worth as much as the others. Nor is it far removed from us even now. We have never been anything other than converted pagans. *"Fiunt, non nascuntur christiani"*, in Tertullian's words; which can be translated: "Pagans are born, but Christians are made". The western way of being a Christian is conditioned by the religious genius of the West. We have a duty to remain faithful to that genius; but we have no business to be foisting it upon others.

There are different ways of being pagan, and each has its own beauty. All deserve to be saved, and all will indeed be saved. It was the semitic way of paganism that was first to be saved, in Abraham. It was the turn of western paganism when Plato and Virgil were, in a sense, baptized. In the twentieth century it will be the turn of African paganism; in the twenty-first, of Indian paganism. Within the unity of a faith which is necessarily one, diversity within Christianity reflects the diversity of the religious outlooks which receive that faith, each in the manner peculiar to itself. And what right have I to impose on other men my own particular way of welcoming Jesus Christ?

Thus one sees how essential it is, if there is to be a firm basis for dialogue, that we be clear about the relationship of Christianity to the other religions. In this matter, as with ecumenism, the fact that love must be operative does not make clarity any less desirable. Nothing whatsoever can be founded on confusion. This is ignored by syncretism, which, by putting everything on the same level, robs dialogue of meaning. The same can be said of sentimentalism, which refuses to mark in watersheds, so to speak, for fear that they become frontiers. One must always state clearly what is the question at issue.

What we have been describing is religion in general. The Judeo-Christian religion confronts us with something quite different. We have not here a system of worship, a cult. What we have is a witness to certain historical events. The Holy Book of the Christians is a history. It states the evidence for the actions of God, where the Word appears in time. One does not have to be a Christian to believe in God. One does have to be a Christian to believe that God has come among men. Religion in general is a turning of man towards God;

revelation bears witness to a turning of God towards man.

The distinctions which arise from this fact are obvious. Religion in general concerns itself with the way in which God manifests his presence through the cycles of nature and of human existence. Revelation is concerned with a unique event, *"hapax"* says the Epistle to the Hebrews. If this event is unique, it is obvious that the revelation concerning it must also be unique. Faith consists in a belief in the reality of that event. On the other hand, other religions must necessarily be diverse, for they are the creations of human genius. They bear witness to the high standards of religious leaders, such as Buddha and Zoroaster, but they must also be marked by the necessary defects of all things human. Revelation is the work of God alone. Man contributes nothing to it, nor does it belong to him. It is a pure gift. It is in itself infallible, true in a sense which can be applied only to God himself.

Religion is concerned in the first instance with the present life. It is one part of natural human existence, even though it expresses the persistence of permanent values. Revelation is eschatological. It is concerned with the last things, with matters which elude man's grasp. It is turned towards the future. It is prophetic. Religion expresses the desire of man for God. Revelation is witness to the fact that God has replied to that desire. Religion does not offer salvation; only Jesus Christ does that. Here, as elsewhere, revelation does not destroy religion but brings it to fulfilment.

Religion is the realm of spiritual experience. It expresses the efforts man makes to develop that part of himself which is turned towards the divine. It will be the richer the better endowed persons are religiously. Revelation is the domain of faith. It does not base itself on a personal experience, but puts its confidence in the experience of another, he who comes from on high and is born in glory. Thus is revelation laid open to the poor. Only faith matters—and grace which acts within man's infirmity.

It is clear, therefore, that if there is opposition between Christianity and other religions, this is not an opposition between realities of the same order which are mutually exclusive. It is rather a sign of a relationship between them. If there is a danger in syncretism, there is a danger no less grave in a radicalism which, in the name of faith, would fail to understand what religion is and what importance it possesses. Such an attitude is very widespread today. People see the destruction of religion as a condition of the faith, and fight against the pagan elements which live on in Christianity. They think that when atheism destroys religion it opens a way for the faith.

Happily, the encyclical *Ecclesiam suam* seems to react against this attitude. While it rejects atheism as a perversion of human nature, it addresses a fraternal appeal to the non-biblical religions. It bears witness at one and the same time to their vitality in the world of today and to the values of which they are the custodians. The position adopted by Paul VI in this matter is the same as that of Pius XII and John XXIII. The encyclical *Evangelii praecones* of Pius XII is particularly important in this connection. It admirably defines the attitude of Christianity to the religious values of paganism. It tells us that Christianity lifts them up, purifies them, and transfigures them.

The three aspects are fundamental.

That Christianity takes up the religious values of paganism and does not destroy them is true theologically. As we have said, Christ comes to take hold of all that is man, and the religious is the most precious part of man. It is true also historically, for although, in a pagan country, Christianity is always at first led to take a stand against the errors of paganism, it goes on to take to itself the good things in it. An obvious example which offers proof of this is the evangelization of the West. Christianity has taken up all that was valuable in the religions of Greece and Rome. Shrines of pagan goddesses became shrines of the Virgin Mary, and the seasonal pagan feasts were displaced by Christmas and Candlemas.

Another aspect of this taking up of the pagan spirit by revelation concerns the diversity of expressions of that spirit. Religious genius takes different forms in different peoples, and Christianity ought to take each variety to itself. Until now it is only the western world that has been evangelized in its culture and therefore also in its religion. And it has come about that the Christianity which the western world has carried to the four quarters of the globe has been a western type of Christianity.

Here we touch on problems of fundamental importance. We are faced today with the rejection of Christianity in the name of their own religion by the peoples of the Far and Near East; and it has to be admitted that this attitude is justified in so far as the Christian revelation is presented to them in the shape in which it has been received by western religious man. What they are rightly rejecting is not Christianity but its western form. For, in this case, it is in fact destructive of the cultural values to which these people have the right and the duty to cling.

A difficulty might legitimately be advanced at this point. It could be objected that the view which has been given of paganism is too optimistic, that the relationship between pagan religions and Christianity is not only that of one adopting what is best in the other, but also that of a breach between the two. Such an objection is perfectly justified. Taken in itself, the religious part of man is an aspect of creation and therefore good. But the religions in which it finds expression in the historical situation are always more or less deformed. These religions, like everything else that is human, belong to a world which is scarred by sin, and they show evidence of it. It is in this sense that they are stumbling-blocks as well as stepping-stones.

This brings us to the second service which, as Pius XII notes, Revelation performs for these other religions. It purifies them. True though it is that God who cannot be seen is adored by pagan men in things which can be seen, it is true also that adoration often stops at the visible things and degenerates into idolatry. This is what St Paul teaches at the beginning of his Epistle to the Romans: "From the foundations of the world men have caught sight of God's invisible nature, his eternal power and his divineness, as they are known through his creatures . . ." But they "exchanged the glory of the imperishable God for representations of perishable man, of bird and beast and reptile" (1, 20, 23). *Romans*

It is true enough that these religions seem to be filled with dark and disquieting elements. Indeed, at times they appear to be privileged haunts for the powers of evil. The Fathers of the Church were not entirely wrong when they saw there devilish forces at work to turn towards themselves the natural movement of men's hearts towards God. Ceremonial is degraded into magic and put at the service of human passions. Superstition takes the place of prayer. A thirst for the marvellous replaces a sense of mystery.

As St Paul saw clearly, from such spiritual depravity strange moral perversions flow : sacred prostitution, infant sacrifice, sexual mutilation.

At their best, these religions can do no more than grope hesitantly for the truth. They can never trace clearly where the frontier lies between God and creature. The greatest of their spiritual leaders do not free themselves of a pantheism which loses God in his universe, and do not succeed in finding a personal and transcendent God. Spiritual experience is sought for its own sake. It does not carry man beyond himself but leaves him to worship that which is best in himself. Nor is there any possibility of understanding the mystery of evil. Either it is reduced to a handicap of which man has to rid himself, or it is seen as existing poles apart from the good, opposing it eternally in a dreadful dialectic.

Thus Christianity makes its influence felt at this level also, although, it must be clearly understood, it stands on quite a different ground. We have already shown in what its specific nature consists. There is, all the same, a relation between it and the values of pagan religions even at this level. It is to this that Pius XII points when he says that Christianity transfigures these religions. It is a fact that the salvation which Christ brings does not put a new reality in place of the reality of nature. The Word comes to save the man whom the Word has made. This man is a religious man. Therefore, it is in his religious values also that the Word comes to transfigure him.

It is easy to show this transfiguration at the different levels at which man's religious bent shows itself. At all these levels, the life of the Holy Spirit comes to take hold of the religious man and introduce him into the life of God himself, where before he had stood outside. As has been said already, pagan man sought God where he showed himself in the signs of nature, that is to say, from outside God, from beyond the gulf set by God's infinite transcendence. But although man cannot cross this abyss, God can. He comes to seek out man in all his littleness, to lift him to himself and introduce him into his very life, into the life of the Trinity.

But the man so brought into the intimacy of God's own life is the same as he who was seeking God in what God had made. Those very things which had served him when he was outside are going now to serve him even better from within. Fire had been the expression of God's purifying power, water of his unifying force, wind of his creative strength; and all these serve now as images of the action of the divine persons. The Spirit is the fire which Christ has come to kindle upon earth, the divine breath which lifts up the Apostles, the living water which flows from the throne of God and of the Lamb.

The human rites which were the points by which the sacred entered in and which awakened in men a longing for they knew not what, have now become the rites which signify the satisfaction of that longing. Henceforth, the new birth that is celebrated is a birth of the spirit and not of the flesh, the awakening of a life which is not the fragile life of the body but the everlasting life of God. The marriage which is celebrated is the union of the Word and mankind which brings to the soul a share in the goods that are divine. The death which comes is no longer the separation of soul from body, but the shuffling off of mortal life to awaken again with Christ.

Quite apart from this, interior experience is part of the human nature of which grace comes to take hold. It is true, of course, that it becomes the greatest of all temptations when it claims to be sufficient in itself, and above all when it considers itself to be superior to faith. On the other hand, if it lays itself open to grace it reaches great heights. For, as Henri de Lubac has said, unless the mysterious becomes mystical and interiorizes itself, it must remain at the level of a merely external faith and formal practice.

This last remark raises two questions of real pastoral importance. We have been saying that there is a reciprocal relationship between Christianity and paganism. Christianity is necessary for Revelation to be fulfilled; but this fulfilment has exactly the same value as has the religious man whom Revelation comes to transform. Thus, Christianity has need of natural religion, just as it has need of all that is truly human, since its only mission is to save that which has first been made.

And so we come back to the problem of the place of the sacred in the contemporary world. Since it is the religious man of whom grace comes to take hold, what will be the case where man is no longer religious, where the sense of the sacred has been lost? When the sun has ceased to be a sign and has become instead only a gigantic nuclear explosion, how is its light to serve as a symbol of the sun of justice, which rises in the East to shine upon the new creation?

Or again, how is a meal to be the sign and sacrament of the communion of Christians with Christ and among themselves, when it has lost the dignity and sacredness it had for men of former times, when it has become only a means of satisfying hunger and is no longer a human rite expressing communion? How is human love to become again the symbol of the love between Christ and his Church, when it is despoiled of its sacredness and mystery and reduced to mere eroticism? How is death, even, to signify the passage to the true life, when euthanasia has taken from it its significance as a personal act of total abandonment into the hands of God?

The featureless cannot be transfigured. An answer can be given only when a question has been asked.

97

Prayer as a Political Problem

The dialogue between Revelation and the world of paganism passes by the problem of religion and atheism, that is to say, the problem of the naturally religious man. It is religion rather than Revelation which is injured in modern man, and that by the folly of those who think that Revelation can dispense with religion. This is the mistake which both Bonhoeffer and Tillich make—and Robinson, also, when he puts their questions. When Revelation is presented to a man who is Godless, it can be understood only as a human device. In this context Jeanson was right to invite Christians to free Christianity from the incubus of God, to cut Revelation adrift from religion.

However, the question is badly put. Or rather, there is no real insight in it. The question is not whether Revelation can or cannot do without the sacred. What we have to ask is where the sacred is to be found. Or better still, for we know that well enough, how to express in the language of today what all too often we continue to try to explain in the idiom of yesterday. Words hold us fast and prevent us from penetrating to what is real.

The holy is always present, but we do not know how to recognize it. And because we cannot recognize it, we are unable to discover the naturally religious man that faith must reach in order to bring him salvation. It is not in the rearguard of the traditionalists but out at the very front of the thrust into new territory

98

that the holy is to be found in the world of today. We shall find it where it has always been, but where to the man of today it will come as a fresh and gleaming discovery. As Teilhard saw clearly, it is in the vanguard of humanity on the march that the need to adore is born again.

Holiness is found again in the world of nature to exactly the degree that science unfolds new depths in it. The sun again becomes a sacred sign as I perceive that it is indeed an enormous atomic explosion and so charged with all the fear this word excites in a human race which feels its small planet at its mercy. Modern man rediscovers the holy in the depths of space and time, which are so much more an image of infinity than the narrow cosmos which yet roused religious consciousness in the men of antiquity.

More important even than this, it is on the plane of human rites that technology reaches its limits and comes up against something of which it cannot dispose, and which, through this mystery of human nature, brings it back again to the mystery of God, in whose image man is made. When technology has to do with man himself, when it comes to the laws of human generation, it comes face to face with human love and with the mystery of a communion of persons, something that cannot be reduced to eugenic or demographic rules. And when it faces death, it meets that which robs it of all its power, for it can in no way

99

respond to the personal significance of death, the final destiny of the human person.

The Christians of tomorrow will have to face a new type of paganism, a religion which is seeking to find itself, rather than an atheism which cannot long survive the boredom it engenders. It is for this new paganism that the Church is looking when it seeks to read the signs of the times. For the signs of the times are those by which God speaks in human nature. Atheism is no more than a transitional phase, a momentary crisis, between the paganism of the rural civilizations of yesterday and the paganism of the industrial civilization of tomorrow. The religious problem of modern man is the paganism of tomorrow. It is to this that the Church ought to find an answer, this that must be taken up, purified, and transfigured, if it is once again to be proved true that a Christian is never other than a pagan on the way to conversion.

This brings us to the second question, the presence of pagan elements in Christianity. There is nothing to be surprised at in this. We have been saying that there has to be a pagan man because Christianity exists to save him. What this means is that there is not and never has been any such person as an absolutely pure Christian. There are only pagans at various stages of conversion. But it can happen—and often has happened—that the properly Christian element may

100

wither and the pagan element become predominant.

For many Christians it is certainly true that Christianity as it is lived becomes something less than its real content requires and degenerates into a sort of paganism. It becomes only a religion. Because they have been born in a Christian country it is by means of Christian rites that they fulfil their human need to give a sacred character to the basic features of human life: birth, marriage, and death. This paganism is superior to other types because it is a purified paganism. All the same, we do well to recognize that very often it is no more than a form of paganism and that the faith which is specifically Christian is lacking.

England

Are we therefore to conclude that this sort of Christianity must be condemned? Hardly. In a world threatened with atheism, the first care must be to defend awareness of sacred things wherever that may be found. That men are not content to dissociate themselves from God in the central acts of their lives shows that there is in them a religious ground in which the faith can grow. We have also to remember that Christianity demands a personal commitment. Religion is connatural to the mass of mankind; and in a Christian country it is to be expected that many should know Christianity as a religion before they discover it as Revelation.

It follows, then, that the tension which is quite normal between paganism and Christianity is not confined solely to the relations between Christianity and the non-Christian religions. It exists within Christianity itself—between Christianity as Revelation and Christianity as religion, between a personal Christianity and a sociological Christianity, between a Christianity of involvement and a Christianity that jogs along. It would be a grave mistake to ignore the importance of this tension, or to reject as unchristian everything which does not involve a personal engagement, or to despise sociological Christianity. Such behaviour would throw back into paganism an immense crowd of people who find in Christianity the satisfaction of their natural need for God in its purest form—and who, furthermore, have there always available for them the seed of the revelation which will bear fruit in some of them.

Let it be repeated, Christianity does not consist in knowing God. Religion suffices for that. Nevertheless, and as a matter of fact, without Christianity the religions of men have not known the true God—or better, they have not known God truly. When a man knows God truly, he has taken an immense step forward; for that knowledge is the fulfilment of his nature, the foundation of his ethics, the heart of his city. The claim of the Church has always been that it brings to men not only the light which Christ has given on the supernatural destiny and last end of man, but light also on man's natural life and the conditions in which he can find earthly happiness. This is something we ought not to forget.

It is because of this that we can speak of Christian religion, as we speak of Christian philosophy, Christian civilization, Christian ethics. We do not mean that Christianity is either a philosophy, or a civilization, or a religion, or a sort of humanism, even of the highest kind. We are well aware that such a statement would be a completely mistaken interpretation. Christianity is primarily something quite different from all that. It is the saving action of God. But it is all that also. Or rather, it allows these human values to reach their full development even before it brings to them a transfiguration enabling them to surpass themselves. It is in this sense that Christianity has exercised an influence on religion, in helping it to become purified and to free itself from its confusions.

But it is also true that even within Christianity the religious element can become degraded. The problem, therefore, is not that of purifying Christianity of its religious element, but of purifying the religious element itself. By this I mean to say that there are many features of popular piety which have their place in Christianity and which the Church has always defended against those who wished to eliminate them—the cult of the Virgin and of the saints, processions and pilgrimages, blessings and exorcisms, medals and scapulars, candles and offerings; and that these features can easily degenerate into superstition and therefore stand in constant need of being purified.

We are thus led to consider the sort of attention which Christianity ought to give to paganism. On the one hand, we become conscious of the complexity of paganism: there are the traditional pagan religions, the neo-paganism of industrial civilization, the paganism which exists within the Church. On the other hand, we perceive its value. In so far as it is natural religion, paganism appears as a dimension of man's existence. It is on this account that it is an element of the temporal common good. It is on this account also that what it presents to Christian salvation is something that has to be saved. It is this which offers to Christianity the gateways by which entry can be made into the non-Christian religions and contact also made with the expectations of the contemporary world. It is with it as a starting-point and with its orientation towards Christianity that a Christian people becomes possible. All this shows how much opposed to the spirit of the mystery of the Incarnation is a false conception of the purity of Revelation in relation to these pagan elements.

VII

The Church and the Modern World

It has been the argument of this book that while the Church has need of civilization, civilization also has need of the Church. Men become aware that when technical progress puts new resources at their disposal it presents them also with the problem of deciding on what view of man's own nature these resources are to be used. They know now that technology cannot of itself solve their problem, and they look to the Church to tell them what is, in the Church's view, the sort of civilization which will best meet the needs of human nature and be best equipped to bring happiness to mankind.

It is consequently necessary for the Church to give a clear statement of its views on this matter. Yet it is not easy, as discussion during the past half-century has shown, to define clearly the Church's position with regard to the development of the earthly city. All too often there has been a wandering to one side or the other; either the preaching of the Gospel has been abandoned and the activity of Christians become entirely a search after temporal good; or Christians have come to occupy themselves with evangelization and neglect their duty of taking a hand in political affairs. There is something in what the Marxists say: Christianity can be in danger of turning men away from social and political activity precisely because it sees that man's destiny lies far beyond any earthly city.

The Church takes the world seriously. By that I mean that man and man's growth are matters on which the Church has a positive view. The Church takes the world seriously because the world is the creation, that is to say the work of God, and because it would be a very odd thing for men to find bad what God finds good. Men are often more squeamish than God and more easily scandalized. They take exception to violence, although violence is one of the ways in which life bursts forth. There is violence in the animal kingdom, and it is inevitable that there should be violence in the development of the city of men. They are shocked by sexuality; yet God has chosen to put there, at the very root as it were of the living being, that which in the human person will blossom into the marvel of truly personal love. God is not shocked by any part of all these riches of life; and it is to this creation that men have to give their assent.

We need to take particular note of the fact that God has made to man a gift of this creation. He has done this so that men can make an inventory of its riches and use them for their own development. God has made a world in which progress, and particularly technical progress, is an authentic aspect of the creation he wanted to have. That is why the Church must first of all tell Christians, and indeed all men, that this world has to be accepted as it is, in all its aspects. The Christian must not turn aside and sulk, preferring always what is past and finding fault with what is present. Such behaviour shows a lack of respect for that which God himself has willed. What God asks of us is to live in this world, to make ourselves part of it. The Vatican Council has said firmly that this acceptance of the world of today in its full reality is something authentically Christian.

However, it is certain also that what constitutes this world is more than the material elements on which it is based. Technical progress creates a certain number of new possibilities at different levels. It affects means of communication, standards of life, extent of culture. But technical progress can never do more than offer possibilities and change environments. All these changes and possibilities must be ambiguous, capable, that is, of being used in man's service or to do him harm.

When we speak of civilization, therefore, we are not speaking only of the conditions which actually obtain in the modern world, for these constitute only

defn

the possibility of civilization, not civilization itself. The truth is that civilization consists in an order of things where the material elements, which come of technical progress, are made to serve the authentic ends of the human person. In other words, civilization contains not only material but also normative elements. Technology can just as well make a barbarism as a civilization. The modern world can perfectly well become a barbaric world; and, with its nuclear reactors and means of communication, more barbaric than were the ancient worlds which achieved incomparable human successes despite their humbler material resources. Developments in ancient Greece, or in the West in the twelfth and thirteenth centuries, were admirable because they used for the development of persons those material resources which they had at their disposal.

We find ourselves at the main point of our enquiry. We are not concerned with the supernatural destiny of man considered in itself. Death and judgement must always be kept in mind, as also must the sociological aspect, but neither one nor the other is the immediate object of our search. What we look for is sited between these two. It is precisely what may be called the earthly city, that which may be defined as the manner in which the elements of civilization are put at the service of human persons. The earthly city consists essentially in the arrangements for using all the available cultural, economic, political, and international resources as the requirements of the human personality demand.

This area of activity is not easy to demarcate precisely, and there is a great deal of misunderstanding with regard to it, particularly in practice. This intermediate sphere, which is of a temporal order and is different from both the material base of civilization and the ultimate destiny of mankind, is for many not easy to understand. Anything which belongs to the natural order, or comes under natural law, or is on a natural level, is met with some reserve.

It may be that in the first instance the reasons for this are philosophical. It is true that in the current of contemporary thought there are two main tendencies to be found. One is positivist. This confines itself to description, accepts only facts, contents itself with sociological surveys and the preparation of good tables of statistics, and seeks to discover constants in the world of actuality. This is a strong tendency, and a good one, for it presents us with the facts without which action cannot be planned; but all the same, it does refuse to go beyond what is purely descriptive. The other tendency I shall call existentialist. Faced with this factual material, it puts the accent on the human person as free, while paying more attention to the subjective human attitude than to the objective

positivism — matter
existentialism — form

Prayer as a Political Problem

conditions in which this attitude seeks expression.

Be that as it may, the city must be assigned its rightful place: it is not the final goal. It is our pride, as Christians, to say that mankind is destined for something other than the building of a perishable city, that we go towards a city which is imperishable, and that men are called to a life beyond that of this world. But this very boast obliges us to give to the earthly city its due place and proper value. We give it this proper value when we see that its function is to provide for the fulfilment of the human person in this mortal life; that is to say, when we see that <u>the purpose of the earthly city is to provide the conditions which will allow human beings to develop themselves to the full.</u>

for civilization

For this, three elements are necessary. First is the <u>utilization of material goods.</u> That men today should die of hunger is an indication of something profoundly wrong in the world. A régime is civilized, properly speaking, only where the material wealth available is put at the disposal of the community of persons. Poverty and hunger should be seen, not simply as resultants of economic circumstances, nor as simple matters of fact, but as something which goes contrary to the very nature of civilization.

② Secondly, civilization supposes that there is friendship between men, that there exists <u>a communion of persons.</u> It is true that the modern world puts us in possession of many means of communication between persons; that there is a degree of economic, political, and international solidarity; that life in our time is much more collectivized and socialized. But all that is *not simply* not enough to create a community. Nor are we to suppose that a society is necessarily a community. Might it not be, rather, that this society of today, such as we find it particularly in the great agglomerations, is the very negation of community, a world in which there is more loneliness than ever existed before?

I am driven to despair at times when I see what our technological civilization is doing in Africa and Asia, in countries where, in spite of poverty, there was more happiness because more friendship. Happiness is to be found much more in frank and open human relations than in growing material wealth. We destroy happiness when we destroy an existing sense of community and put nothing in its place. There, then, is our second task: to make use of the means of communication at our disposal today—which are altogether admirable— to bring about a wider and closer fellowship among men and to turn the collectivity into a community.

Finally, unless we relate all things to God, neither (3) man nor city can survive. For relationship to God is a constitutive part of human nature as such, and therefore also a constitutive part of the earthly city as such; and this quite anterior to any ordering to a future world and a supernatural life. It is natural man who is directed towards God by the very fact of his nature.

III

Therefore, when Christians defend God's place in the city as being an essential element of the city, it is not God whom they defend—he has no need of anybody's defence and is not even threatened—but man himself.

Two things are necessary: that men live in fellowship with each other, and that they live in communion with God; and it may be that Christians have betrayed their calling at times because they have not said firmly enough that, for them, the two commandments are absolutely inseparable. A world in which men cannot be at home is an inhuman world; and so is a world in which God is not at home. Christians, and all other men of good will, can be called the servants of love only when they have the courage to proclaim before all the world that there is no civilization other than this, and that to build it they will dedicate all their strength; for this is the one city which conforms to the requirements of human nature.

Let us consider the application of this in the contemporary world, looking at what the Council, using a phrase of John XXIII, has called the "signs of the times." Some of these signs are positive, and it is in these that the Church recognizes the voice of God. It is God himself who uses these to put his questions; and hence the dialogue between the Church and the world is a dialogue of God with himself. It is God who speaks through the Church and God also who speaks through the world. There is no question of a dialogue between God and something which is foreign to him. The Council says exactly this, that progress is an expression of God's creation, that it is God who is hidden in it, and that we must know how to find him there.

It must be clearly understood that what we are concerned with in the first instance is technical progress itself. An outstanding characteristic of our world is the use of applied science to bring about an incredibly rapid transformation of the conditions in which men live. Equally important is the fact that men are becoming conscious of their unity. This comes about because, on the one hand and negatively, they find themselves for the first time threatened all together—we know now that we could all be swept away at one blow and to that extent our destiny is common; and because, on the other hand and positively, all are called to live through the beginnings of the same great adventure— and one which makes them very conscious of the unity of their species—the expansion of the earth into the cosmos.

Another important feature of the time is the recognition of adulthood in every sort of man. Until now many men could not share fully in the goods of civilization because they could not play a full part in its constitution. The workers—one of the oldest and most striking of emancipations—are having a more and more effective voice in economic affairs. The non-European peoples are being freed from colonialism and are taking an equal place among the nations. Women are playing a more adult role in those fields which are particularly their own and also in economic life and in politics. These were all indicated by John XXIII. I would add to them the increasing importance of youth, for there is today increasing pressure from the young to intervene more directly in those questions which concern them.

But—and here I come to the negative elements—it is plain that all this does not suffice to make a civilization. It might equally well make a barbarism which could end in chaos. In other words, nothing of this can have any value except to the extent that we are building a world which is truly human. There is evidence enough that we are not making much progress and have made many blunders, for the world is full of grave disorders. In this situation the Church has to point to those things which are bad in the world and indicate how they ought to be dealt with. For to say "yes" to the world does not imply that we have to accept indifferently everything we find in the world, whether it comes from God or the devil.

One can be up-to-date by saying yes, or by saying no. To be truly a man of one's own time one must know how to love all that the world offers that is positive, and at the same time hate all that is by human malice compromised and destroyed—and this because one loves one's world and all who live in it. All that has a positive value can be turned into a negative. Technical progress can be used to suppress the spiritual side of men, by tempting them to concentrate entirely on material production and in doing so sacrifice the essential part of themselves. Such a concentration of all efforts on production of material goods is a pressing danger which threatens man's mutilation.

I have said that mankind is moving towards unity, but I would add that such a movement would be bad if unification led to uniformity, and thus to the destruction of one of the most precious possessions of humanity—the rich diversity of its cultures. An integral humanism would be one to which Africa, China, America, and the old countries of Europe brought each their own languages, cultures, and outlooks. What each has to offer, once lost, could never be replaced. It was André Gide who remarked that a writer was the more universal the more firmly he was embedded in his own country. "There is nobody more English than Shakespeare and no one more universal; none more Italian than Dante and no one more universal; none more French than Racine and no one more universal." To destroy these differences at the very moment when the young nations of Africa and Asia are rediscovering them with joy would be a crime against culture and against humanity. There is undoubtedly all too great a danger today of bringing everything to one level.

How dreadfully monotonous and wearisome would be a culture of *homo technicus* which was exactly the same in Pekin as in Buenos Aires or London or Dakar!

There is something admirable in this movement in which all men claim to be recognized as men, all as equals, all as adult. Nevertheless, if this urge towards freedom leads men to declare their independence of God, to set themselves up as sovereign, to chafe at the necessity of having to recognize that there is one who is greater than themselves, they will fail to see that, while at the human level all men are truly equal, what alone guarantees their freedom and dignity is the presence of a power beyond them to which they can appeal, of a love greater than any they can compass, of a good which is truly supreme; and when they fail thus, the drive to emancipation, which is admirable in itself when properly expressed, must become destructive of their fundamental values in cutting away the most essential part of themselves, their relation to an Absolute.

There is one more step to take. This is to show in what the mainspring of the temporal activity of the Christian consists, and why the duty of temporal action comes directly out of the nature of Christianity and is demanded by the Christian's fidelity to God. It has to be shown that in this activity he works out his salvation and on this activity he will be judged, so that, even

116

though he pray morning and night, if he fail in it he fails in his duty as a Christian.

The majority of Christians are quite convinced still that a man can perfectly well work out his eternal salvation while being completely uninterested in political affairs. This must be stated plainly. The cause lies partly in a faulty formation of conscience. Not nearly enough of an effort has been made to get people to take seriously their duty of serving the earthly city. Part also of the cause lies in the difficulty of maintaining both that it is a fundamental tenet of Christianity that the earthly city is not the final goal and the Christian has to look to more than its construction; and that this doctrine does not at all mean that participation in the earthly city's affairs is not a grave duty for the Christian nor one from which he can dispense himself.

It has, then, to be demonstrated why the duty of building the earthly city proceeds directly from the demands of the Christian conscience. We have only to look at God's word, at the fundamental teaching which we find in the Scriptures. Isaiah, Jeremias, Amos were assiduous in denouncing injustices and in occupying themselves with international problems. I know of no stronger text against inequality in the ownership of material goods—and this touches on one of the three essential conditions for the existence of a real civilization—than this passage from Isaiah: "Woe upon you, that must ever be acquiring house after house, field after neighbouring field, till all the world goes wanting!" (5.8.) The situation then was one of accumulation in the hands of some and despoliation of others; and there has never been a stronger protest against or a more realistic description of that enrichment and impoverishment.

The prophets never ceased from their interventions. Why? Renan saw Amos as the first demagogue. Marx saw in the Old Testament prophets the first protagonists of the class war. A close reading of the texts shows that such explanations as these are completely false. It is a great contemporary Jewish philosopher, André Neher, who shows that the prophet Amos denounced injustices precisely because he was speaking in the name of God. The charter for the earthly city is found in the alliance between Yahweh and his people. That charter is always being violated by men, and particularly by those of them who are rich and powerful. The role of the prophet is continually to denounce these violations of the Alliance, to recall to men's minds what is God's law in the earthly city, and thus to set in train some concrete action against the breaches of it. All this is done out of allegiance to God, and not in virtue of something with which he has no concern.

This, then, is the definitive answer to the question with which we began. When, whether in unions, politics, or cultural matters, a Christian becomes wholly involved in struggles to bring the earthly city into conformity with its charter, or, what is the same thing, with the true ends of man, he does not quit God nor God's sanctuary to lose himself in a foreign world, as all too often he is led to think. It is true that this domain of the earthly city is a world of hard fighting, where the Christian often feels himself lost amid the tumult and the passion, the whirlpool of false ideas and the clashing of ambitions. It is true that the Christian might well feel some repugnance against involvement with this terrible world, because he fears, and not without reason, that he might there lose his soul. Nevertheless, it would be a tragic mistake if he refused to share in men's struggles because he wanted to preserve his peace of mind.

Therefore it is necessary for him to realize that the call to struggle comes from God himself in the midst of this earthly city which is subject to his law, and which he wants to see conform to it. When the Christian, having prayed, flings himself into the battle, he finds that he has left God in order to meet God again. The Christian cannot let himself be deceived by a false laicism which sees the realities of political and economic life as belonging to a completely profane world existing apart from God. Of course, there is a distinction of powers, and this world is not subject directly to the authority of the Church. But to say that this world is not directly subject to the Church's authority is not to say that it is not subject to the law of God, of which the *magisterium* of the Church is the interpreter.

If only the Christian understands that when he serves the earthly city he serves God and his brethren, and that when he works at the building of the earthly city he moves towards his own eternal salvation, he will be able to bring to his mind the words of Jesus: "He who gives a glass of water to one of these little ones, gives it to me." And if he takes these words of Jesus in a wider sense, and goes beyond the individual act of charity to that modern form of charity which consists essentially in the service of civilization through its institutions, he will be in process of saving his soul. It is Christ himself who assures him of it. To serve one's brothers and to save one's soul are not opposed one to the other; they are one and the same thing. In doing what needs to be done, the Christian can rediscover the unity of his vocation, of his being, and of his personality.

Conclusion

THE point from which the argument of this book began was the danger in which Christianity stands of becoming a small sect of the elect and ceasing to be the religion of the poor. We have argued that this must inevitably be so in a civilization which finds no place for the religious dimension of man. This has led us to ask what is the essential nature of civilization. It has become clear that it is of the essence of civilization to allow man to reach his full development, and that this development applies also to the religious dimension. Thus we have come to see that the problem facing us is the problem of religion as a constitutive element of civilization.

The affirmation that religion is important is today contested not only by atheistic ideologies, but also by the "secularist" doctrines which reject the sacred character of earthly realities and activities, and split the temporal away from the spiritual. This "secularism" shows itself at the level of the material universe, which is seen exclusively as a network of physical relations and not in its ontological dimension of creation. It shows itself also at the social level by its refusal to treat religion as a social factor in the city in course of development.

This secularism not only creates conditions which make the survival of the Christian people impossible, but also endangers civilization itself. The Council takes a stand against it in the Constitution *Gaudium et Spes*. While accepting the autonomy of scientific disciplines and methods, the Council insisted that the things which form their subject-matter—the physical universe, the human person, economic and political society—belong entirely to God.

It will suffice here to quote a few passages. "It is obviously false to maintain that the temporal is autonomous if by that we mean that created things do not belong to God and that man can dispose of them without reference to his Creator. . . . All believers, whatever their religion, have always seen God's presence manifested in the language of his creatures" (par. 36, 3). And again : "It is from God that man receives everything : he sees all things as springing from the hand of God and respects them" (par. 37, 4). It can be said that what the Council here sets down is the essence of religion, the recognition that everything is the gift of God.

It is not only faith which the Church defends, but also reason, nature, and the truth about man. Of course, the religious man of tomorrow will express himself in ways different from those used yesterday.

The problem is one of interpretation. We do not seek to empty of meaning words like God, sin, religion, or to secularize them by giving them a sense which is entirely profane. On the contrary, what we try to do is to express their objective content, starting from the experience of contemporary man.